SILVERTOWN

SILVERTOWN

An East End Family Memoir

Melanie McGrath

FOURTH ESTATE • *London*

First published in Great Britain in 2002 by
Fourth Estate
A division of HarperCollins*Publishers*
77–85 Fulham Palace Road
London w6 8jb
www.4thestate.com

2 4 6 8 10 9 7 5 3 1

A catalogue record for this book is available from
the British Library

ISBN 1-84115-142-4

Typeset by Rowland Phototypesetting Ltd,
Bury St Edmunds, Suffolk
Printed in Great Britain by
Clays Ltd, St Ives plc

In memory of my grandparents,
Jenny Fulcher and Leonard Stanley Page

Out of the strong came forth sweetness

Judges 14 and motto of Lyle's Golden Syrup

Preface

You could say that Jenny Fulcher led a very ordinary life. She grew up, worked, married and had children. Her life was subject to the usual disquiets and worries. She fretted over her debts. She worried for the future. Every so often, lying in bed in the flat dawn light, she would wonder what the point of all the struggle was. And then she would get up and make a pot of tea and get on with it. Sometimes a voice in her head whispered that she was a bad wife and a poor mother. Other times the voice soothed and said she had done her best. From time to time, she wondered if anyone had ever really loved her. A few small comforts kept her going: tinned red salmon, cheap perfume and the scandal stories in *Reveille* magazine. She loved TV soaps and flowers – freesias and violets in particular. She knitted and sewed patchwork and converted the results into tea cosies. Over the nine decades of her life she made enough tea cosies to cover all the teapots of England.

It was the kind of life that could have belonged to a thousand women living in the mid years of the twentieth century in the East End of London. Except that it didn't. It belonged to Jenny.

Jenny's turn in the world began in 1903 in Poplar. The death of Queen Victoria two years earlier had ended an era, but remnants of the old century persisted. Women still wore corsets and horses still pulled hackney carriages. The streets still mostly unlit and as slippery as a snake pit. The East End had a grim reputation, and for the most part it was deserved. In the same year Jenny was born, Jack London visited the place and wrote a book about what he saw. He called it *People of the Abyss*.

My grandmother Jenny grew up in that Abyss. To be an East Ender then was to be among the lowest of London's poor, but Jenny never thought of herself as low. To Jenny, there was only respectable and common and by her own account she was respectable. This had nothing to do with money – no one in the East End had much of that; it had to do with blood and conduct.

Jenny was salty and wilful, as thin and prickly as the reeds that once grew where she was born. Her heart was full of tiny thorns, which chafed but were never big enough to make her bleed. Vague feelings drifted about her like mist: bitterness, resentment and rage, mostly. Life was as much a mystery to her as she was to herself. She'd spend hours plotting how to squeeze an extra rasher from the butcher, but on the bigger issues she was helpless. She grasped the details without understanding anything of the general rules. She never had the means to manage her life and so was destined to be bent in the shape of desires, urges and ambitions greater than her own.

All the same, when her face lit up it was like a door swinging out into sunshine. There was something irrepressibly naughty about her. You'd imagine her standing behind your back poking her tongue out at you. She revelled in playing the martyr but was comically bad at the part. She'd insist on giving you the last piece of cake, then reach into her handbag when she thought you weren't looking, pull out a huge bar of chocolate, stuff it in her mouth all at once and pretend she had a cough and couldn't talk. Her luxuriant moaning had to be witnessed to be believed. On bad days everything from her kidneys to her knitting cost too much, ached like geronimo or was doing its best to rip her off.

No life is without its joys, though, and Jenny Fulcher harboured two great passions. The first of these was the crystallised juice of an Indian grass, *Saccharum officinarum L.*, otherwise known as sugar. She favoured the bleached, processed, silvery white stuff, in crystal form or cubes. She spooned it into her tea in extravagant quantities and whenever she thought no one was looking, she'd lick a bony finger, dunk it in the sugar bowl and jam it into her mouth. She was partial to biscuits, cakes, marmalade, tarts and chocolate too, but sweets were really her thing. Over the course of her life, thousands of pounds of Army and Navy tablets, barley sugars, candyfloss, Everton mints, Fox's glacier mints, humbugs, iced gems, jellies, liquorice comfits, Mintoes, nut brittle, orange cremes, pralines, Quality Street, rhubarb and custards, sugared almonds, Toblerone and York's fruit pastilles, met their sticky end on my grandmother's sweet tooth. Sugar was both lover and friend. It had the capacity to seduce, and also to keep her company. Her life went sour so quickly she relied on sugar to lend it sweetness. Sugar was the only thing she had the courage to make a grab for. Even after her hearing went she was never quite deaf to the rustling of humbug wrappers. When her sight failed she could still spot a Fry's Chocolate Crème bar lying on a table top.

Though she didn't realise it, my grandmother's other great love was the East End. She moaned about it constantly – the cramped streets with their potholed pavements, the filthy kids and the belching factories – but she hated the thought of leaving, even for a day. She rarely ventured west and seldom troubled herself with whatever lay on the other side of the Thames. Her list of disgruntlements was long but she never really hankered to be anywhere else. The East End was a mother to her, and she had no means to imagine herself without it. She gave up her health for sugar but she gave up everything else for the East End.

Jenny Fulcher had a husband, my grandfather Leonard. He was not one of her passions. On the surface, they didn't even have much in common. She was the product of the low-lying lanes and turnings of Poplar, where the Thames coils into a teardrop. He came from the sodden terrain of mud and reeds further to the east, from a hamlet sprinkled over the flat fields and rush beds of southern Essex. He was the son of a farm labourer, she the daughter of a journeyman carpenter. She grew up among the factories and tenements sandwiched between the Thames and the West India Docks. He passed his childhood among clouds and a sweep of cabbage fields.

All the same, they shared something beyond the everyday. There was something of the east of England about them both. Their beginnings were bogged down in poverty, their prospects tarnished and their horizons low. They began life on the flat. For years they both looked up at the world, and the world, in its turn, looked down on them.

On the surface, Len Page was all charm and muscular wit. Anyone who didn't care to look too hard would see a diamond bloke, smartly kitted out, with a military swing to his step. People said he was a bit of a laugh. A right old type. In fact he was several types at once. The guv'nor, the back-slapper, the all-round card, but also the trickster, the slippery fish, the spiv. To tell the truth, Len Page was whatever type would get him where he wanted to go. He was as ambitious as the weeds that push up through concrete. To watch him closely was to watch the hatching and execution of unspoken plans.

Len also had two passions: the country and a woman called June. But there will be time for them later.

PART ONE

CHAPTER I

Poplar was built on the back of the sea trade. About six hundred years ago, the place was marked by a single tree standing on lonely marshes and pointing the ancient route from London to Essex. The loops of the Thames at Limehouse Reach in the west and Blackwall Reach in the east protected the area from the worst of the river floods, and in 1512 the East India Company took advantage of its sheltered position to establish a ship-building business at the eastern edge. Very soon after, houses went up on the sloppy soil, craftsmen moved in, then shopkeepers. Oakum merchants arrived, followed by gluemakers, ironmongers, outfitters, manufacturers of naphtha, turpentine, creosote, varnish, linen, tar, timber boards, linseed oil and rubber goods, and Poplar became a town of ropemakers and sailmakers, chandlers, cauterers, uniform-makers, seamen, carpenters, ships' engineers and, of course, ships.

Poplar was once a place that counted. It was from Brunswick Wharf on its eastern edge that the Virginia Settlers sailed. In 1802 the East India Company, frustrated by the small size of the upstream docks and wharves in the London Pool beside the Tower, carved out two spectacular corridors of impounded water, the East and West India Docks, one on each side of the mouth of the Isle of Dogs. Two-masted tea clippers, brigantines, colliers, packet boats, screw steamers, schooners, riggers, cutters, whalers, wool clippers,

3

shallops, four-masters, dromonds, barges and lighters moored at the quays and wooden dolphins of these broad new docks, half-sunk with barrels of molasses, boxes of bananas, silk, pineapples, parrots, spices, tea, rice, sugar, grain, coffee, cocoa mass, ballast, monkeys, macaws, ivory, alabaster, basalt and asbestos, and discharged their cargoes safely into the warehouses inside the dock walls. It was a great time for trade and the East and West India Docks grew so fast that the bigger ships, the tea clippers and steamers, often found themselves moored for as long as a month at mid-stream anchor, waiting their turn to discharge.

My grandmother's ancestors were tidal people, Huguenots who were washed first into the East End then into Poplar during the persecution of Protestants by Catholics in France in the 1680s. Afraid for their lives, they sailed up the Thames and found sanctuary in East London. Many gathered in Spitalfields near the City walls; others fanned out among the numerous little villages along the river, hoping to lie low for a while then move back to France once the troubles were done. But over the years of their exile their number multiplied and they stayed. Fuelled by the frantic energy of immigrants with something to prove, they evolved quite naturally into entrepreneurs, working as ragmen, clothiers, silk spinners and dyesmen. At Spitalfields they built silk weaveries and found a way to fix scarlet dye into silk which they then sold back to Catholic cardinals for robes. For more than a hundred years the River Lea ran red with their labours.

They developed English habits and their names gradually Anglicised, but after three hundred years you could still spot an East Ender with Huguenot blood. Take Jenny Fulcher. She was tiny, sallow, with the horse-brown hair of southern women. Her skin would only have to see the sun to turn brick brown. It was an embarrassment to her family. Fer gawd's sake git some powder on yer face, you're as black as a woggie-wog, her mother, Sarah, would say whenever the summer came. Having no money for powder, Jenny would salt her skin with bicarb of soda, because there was nothing worse than looking foreign (except *being* foreign, which was unthinkable).

Poplar is a mess these days. It has lost its civic quality and become little more than a scattering of remnants and cheap offcuts sliced through by the rush of the East India Dock Road and the Northern Approach to the Blackwall Tunnel. The workhouse has gone, and the East India Dock, but if you look carefully, what remains tells a story about how Poplar used to be. At the bottom of Chrisp Street, where a very fine market once stood, the monolithic pile of the Poplar Baths still stands, though the building is derelict and sur-rounded by razor wire. Along the High Street, between the new-build housing developments and shabby Sixties shopping parades, there remain the architectural remnants of Poplar's marine and trading past: a customs house, some ancient paintwork advertising a chandlery, an old seamen's mission. Further east on the Tunnel Approach, the magnificent colonnades of Poplar Library gather dirt from the traffic and its boarded up windows furnish irresistible spaces for taggers and graffiti artists.

By the time Jenny (or Jane, as she was then) is born, Poplar has become filthy and overcrowded, a victim of its own success. Those who can afford it have moved out to more spacious environs further from the dock walls. My great grandfather, John Fulcher, or Frenchie as he was known, his wife, Sarah, and their children live in Ullin Street, between the Cut and the River Lea. Ullin Street is near to Frenchie's place of work, the Thames Ironworks at Orchard Place. Poplar is jammed with terraces of shabby lets and subdivisions put up by speculators as housing for dockworkers. There are a hundred, even a thousand similar streets stacked along the eastern flank of the city like so much left luggage. They are ugly, redoubtable places, but by no means the worst the East End has to offer.

If you are born there, the docks are the language you speak, the smells you know, the ebb and flow of your life. And so it is with Jane. She grows up beside queues of drays, moving slowly towards the dock gates; beside the twice-daily rush of men struggling to find day work; beside the crush of seamen and foreigners, their strange languages breaking from beneath turbans, yellow faces, pigtails, ice-blue eyes. Jane is aware of the tidal pull of the water before she can even read the tide tables flyposted on the sides of every public house in Poplar. The phalanxes of Port of London Authority policemen, the pawn shops, the bold glances of loose women, the rat nests and dog fights, the boozed-up sailors of a Saturday night, the bustling tradesmen, the drinking dives and gambling holes, the deals made, the greetings and the farewells, the dockers' pubs and pawnbrokers and seamen's missions: all these are familiar to her.

In 1903 the Fulcher family are living in the upper two rooms at number 4 Ullin Street. At the southern end of the street sits the bulking, red brick mass of St Michael and All Angels church and beside it, a gloomy vicarage set in a dark little garden. The remainder of the street is lined with poky terraces where it is common for families of seven or eight to be packed into a single room. There are men in Ullin Street who are forced to work night shifts because there is nowhere for them to sleep until their children have gone to school and the beds are free. And not unskilled labourers either, but craftsmen and artisans. The 1891 census shows sailmakers, foundrymen, glass blowers and carpenters, all living on Ullin Street.

Having two rooms between them, the Fulchers are among the more fortunate. The larger of these rooms is an imperfect square of about twelve feet containing an iron bedstead with an ancient

6

horsehair mattress where Frenchie, Sarah and the younger children sleep, a large fireplace in which a coal stove burns whenever there is money for coal, a gas lamp, a table fashioned by Frenchie from fruit crates, a decaying wicker chair and two fruit crate stools. The room is for the most part mildewy and cheerless, smelling of the family's activities: cooking, bathing, smoking and sex. It is rarely warm enough to open the window and the wooden sashes have in any case swollen with damp and stuck in their frames, though the draught still sails into the room like an unwanted relative. During the autumn and winter Sarah has to lay newspaper over the panes to keep the cold out, and for six months of the year the family live more or less in darkness, the gas lamp on the wall having been deemed an extravagance they can do without.

The second room is much smaller, little more than a box really, and houses another horsehair mattress which has to be shaken of its bedbugs every morning and rolled into a bolster to serve as a seat and a table. All but the youngest of the children, as well as an older female cousin, sleep on this mattress, and though the room has no fire, its small size and busy population keep it warm. In keeping with their relative sizes, Frenchie and Sarah's room is known as Main Room and this second room Little Room. On occasion, when there is no money for coal or even for a bucket of coal dust, the whole family is obliged to move into Little Room just to keep from freezing.

Downstairs live another family, the Smileys – Jack, Violet and their nine or so children, the number varying according to whether there is a new arrival that year to balance the one or two carried off by the whooping cough or TB. The Smileys are permanently unlucky. If there is a bout of pneumonia going around, then one of the Smileys is bound to get it. If a neighbour's boy runs amok with a football, then it will be the Smileys' window which gets broken.

If the vicar is doing his rounds, he'll always knock first on the Smileys' door.

Jack Smiley works as a hatchman in the East India and his wife takes in washing and sometimes cleans the ships' galleys at the East India, but it is never enough. The tallyman is a regular visitor at the Smiley residence. So is the rent collector. And the bookies' boy. Every Monday morning you can set your watch by the appearance of the Smiley children lumbering up the pavement carrying the family sheets and coats to Nathan James Ltd, outfitter and pawn-broker, where they will remain until Friday payday.

The Smileys and the Fulchers share a small concrete back yard with a privy and a standing tap, from where the Fulchers take their water. The privy is a dirty business. In the summer the smell draws egg-filled bluebottles and in the winter the wind sneaks in and freezes their buttocks to the seat. At some point during the previous decade the privy door worked part-way off its hinges leaving a gap the size of a toddler's hand. But for all that, the plumbing is solid, there are rarely any overspills or seeping pipes, and most of the rats stay away. For those that don't, the Smileys' liver-coloured mongrel Bobs does a grand job of disposal, leaving rat tails and other remnants about as proof of his efficacy.

Frenchie Fulcher works as a ships' carpenter at Thames Ironworks on Bow Creek, and sometimes at the West India dry dock. He is a journeyman without a permanent job and has to shape up each morning before seven in the hope that the foreman at the Ironworks has room for him. If not, he'll go down to the West India and try to pick up something there. Fulcher is not a heavy man. All the same, he is an angry man and his neat little body conceals the strength of horses. Among dockers with their sloping shoulders, their rickety legs and half-broken backs, Frenchie the carpenter appears upright and dignified. His manner, too, sets him apart. Men less fastidious than Frenchie go to lengths at shape up, laying on their Irish/Polish/Scots origins and playing the blue-eyed boys. But French is above all that. If there is no work on any particular day, he will go home empty-handed and take it out on the kids. He is proud that way.

On a day when he is feeling right with the world Frenchie looks almost regal. His features are neat and well-made: a slender nose, domed a little in the middle but with a thin pinch at the end; wide-set, peaty eyes with a good measure of white in them, the kind of eyes in which daydreams have space to hide; and a generous but not excessive forehead — a testament, so Sarah says, to his good blood. His voice is high but his laughter, when it comes, is unexpectedly deep and clanging, not unlike an anchor dropping on its chain.

Sarah Fulcher is Frenchie's opposite, a coarse-grained, flap-fleshed woman of wholesome temperament. She is pliant and sweet, with no obvious vices and a handy array of virtues ranging from dress-making to midwifery. Most important of all, Sarah Fulcher is thrifty. She can sniff out a rotten swede or a poor potato at ten yards. No Chrisp Street costermonger will dare to slink a slimy cabbage or dud carrot into Sarah's bag because they know her shrieks of latherish rage will echo halfway to the Thames Estuary. Taking money from Sarah Fulcher's hand is as hard as prising the ring off a rigor mortised finger.

This small reservoir of fierceness is all the more remarkable because in other ways Sarah Fulcher is soft as snow. Her skin is soft and her hair is soft. Her ears have a wispy bloom of hair and fudgy lobes. Her body is as spongy as sausage meat, her lips as plump as spring chicks. Her disposition, too, is spring-like, fresh, sunny and innocent. A little insensitive, even undigested, but never, ever cruel. So sweet is she that the Smiley children all wish she were their mother, because, unlike Mrs Smiley, Sarah only thumps her children when she can't think of any other way to make them do what they are told.

Sarah's love for Frenchie is sweetly naïve and unshakeable. Her life is divided into two eras: Before and After Frenchie. Before Frenchie, Sarah Quelch toiled in a scullery for a family Up West. The family was miserable and the scullery was worse. Then Sarah met Frenchie, married him and found herself living in the bright new world of After Frenchie. In the wide open spaces of Sarah's mind Frenchie is a kind of a god, or at the very least, a saviour. So unquestioning is Sarah's devotion that she seems not to sense her husband's deep sighs, his eyes rolled to the heavens. In an obscure corner of his heart Frenchie resents her. Resents his children, too. The wastefulness of them! The toiling that has to be done to keep them all from the poorhouse. Without Sarah and her brood of guzzling children just think where Frenchie might have ended up! As the owner of a timber yard, perhaps, or a chandler's, or a leather business, or even a cabinetmaker's shop. Occasionally, when he has had too much to drink, he'll give voice to his disappointments, but Sarah only smiles at that and blows him a kiss and says, San Fairy Ann, dear, San Fairy Ann, and he will give up trying to explain.

Sarah gives birth to seven children: William, Rosetta, Frances Maud, John, Jane, Edith and Arthur. The eldest, William, is born premature and doomed. He survives for two days and his body is buried without ceremony in the cemetery not far from Ullin Street. (Rosetta does not grow to adulthood either, but we'll come back to her.) William is never mentioned and the remembrance of him surfaces only occasionally as a faraway look in Sarah's eye or a twitch on Frenchie's face, and so Jane is born into a family with a missing part. No photograph of William exists, no sketch or representation of any kind. It is almost as though his very absence is shameful and must not be acknowledged. But acknowledged it is, of course. When Jane is about five or six, she comes across a wooden soldier wrapped in a piece of old sheeting and hidden at the back of the cupboard beside the fire. It is a beautifully carved, old-fashioned kind of soldier with painted eyes and woollen hair and a red wooden jacket around his broad shoulders and Frenchie's mark carved into his base, and from then on the soldier is William, a little wooden brother who lives in a cupboard and will never grow up.

The Fulcher children are not the most handsome brood. Edie gets most of the looks: arched eyebrows, deep blue eyes and a mouth made from strawberry jam. Jane's older sister Frances Maud, her older brother John and younger brother Arthur are like their mother, squashy and bovine and big-nosed. Only Rosie and Jane take after their father, though Rosie has inherited her mother's soft outlines. By contrast, Jane is a tiny, reedy thing, with bones as skinny as a shrew's. A meagre, curved nose juts from cheeks that would these days be prized, but in those days simply emphasised her thinness. The zooming eyes are a lively blue, though apt to be inspecting. The teeth are good and even. There is nothing wrong with any of her features. It's just that when put together they are uneventful.

What does stand out is Jane's extraordinary hair, a huge, mobile clump of mahogany brown, so soft that it sails in the wind like a bank of seaweed under waves. I'll say one thing for her, says Frenchie, shaking his head, she musta bin standing in the giant's line when the hair was given out. It looks more like an explosion than a bonce.

Mum, where's the End in East End?

The Docks, Janey love, the Docks is the End. The East End is the Docks.

But Mum, where's the Beginning then?

Oh Janey, Janey, the questions you ask! How should I know? You knew where the Finish was.

But it's harder to say where the Beginning is. Ain't no East Beginning s'far as I know. There's only an East End.

In Poplar, the day is divided not into twenty-four hours but into the two shifts of the tides. Since this isn't so much a practical circumstance as a feeling, it would be more accurate to say that the day is divided into two feelings. A kind of thickness in the air signals high tide. Low tide has the sapping quality of a rainy Sunday afternoon. When the river is low the air is thinner and pulls on the hairs of the skin. As the tide rises, do does the mood; as it falls, the mood falls too.

Aside from this dependence on the tides, the typical Fulcher family day is like that of any other poor London family. Morning begins at dawn when the knocker-up wakes Sarah and Frenchie and the babies with a pebble at the window. Rising from the bed, Sarah goes downstairs to the tap by the privy to fetch water for Frenchie's shave and, lighting three coals with a handful of kindling, she boils in the copper three tin cupfuls for the shave and a further eight for tea, before waking the children in Little Room. A child is despatched with two pennies and a tin jug to Neal Charles' dairy in Cottage Place, where there is an outside pump in the shape of a cow's head. While her husband scrapes his beard, Sarah slices half a loaf from the day before and spreads it with dripping or jam for the older children and soaks a little in sugared milk for the toddlers. If there are leftovers from the day before, then Sarah will fry them up for Frenchie. They eat on their laps with their breath pooling in the cold air of the room, the younger ones sipping warm sugary water, the older ones washing down their bread with sweet tea from the tin mug.

At six-thirty Frenchie joins the procession of men heading south towards the docks to the bomp-on for work, men in quiet waves, whistling against the cold. The Fulchers will not see him again till teatime at seven, or if it is a Friday, not till he rolls in from the pub singing 'Mother Brown'. A little later the coal man, the beigel man, the cat's meat man, the haberdasher, the tinker, the pie man and the rag and boner begin making their way along St Leonard's Road, while in the neighbouring streets, doors fly open and women spill out on to the pavement, their hair all done in rags and curlers, eyes beady for a bargain.

Back at Ullin Street, the children scrub their necks and faces at the tap in the yard then the older ones sling on their jackets and head towards the red brick box at Bright Street, which serves as a school. By midday they will be back for lunch, to warmed rooms smelling of their mother's chores. After school the girls will be sent out to fetch saucers of pickles or an egg or two from the grocer's and the boys will be sent to the coal yard for coal dust at a farthing a bucket to make the coals go further. Then Frenchie will sail home hard and sweating from the day, a pilfered orange or a few raisins in his pocket. Look what old Frenchie found in the docks, nippers. Sarah will make sweet tea and put a new half-loaf on the table with marg and jam. Sometimes they will have a few potatoes with gravy or a hard-boiled egg with vinegar pickles and then, unless it is raining very hard or the cold is unbearable or they are sick, the children will play in the street — rope games, ginger, blind man's bluff. Frenchie will sink into his dilapidated chair with his *Daily Mirror* and quarter ounce of shag and shake his head at the injustices of the world, while his wife sits beside him, mending rips and holes. And when the children are in bed and their overcoats are spread over their warming toes, Frenchie will tell them stories.

Frenchie's head is a cargo of stories. He'll tell them about the docker who was pushed into the oily water by a side of beef swung from a ship, and how his fellows made a fire right there on the quayside and roasted that side of beef in tribute to their lost friend. He'll tell them about the parrots which came in on a boat from Uruguay and swore in fourteen different languages, or about the performing monkeys which could write the alphabet. He'll tell them tales of everyday life on the docks. He'll tell them about the sugar porters whose flesh is so raw from the sharpness of their cargo that the bluebottles get in underneath their skin and lay their eggs. How on a summer's day you can tell a sugar porter by the clouds of tiny flies bursting from his limbs. He'll tell them about the tarantulas they pull from banana hands, scooping them up into tobacco tins to give them to their dogs to kill. He'll tell them about the oilmen, whose skin is like thick, black leather from the tar they scrape from the inside of the oil ships, about the potash haulers with faces white as ghosts coughing bloody spume into cloths; about the corn porters with their flour rashes and the sulphur men whose hair stinks of rotten eggs.

Frenchie knows things. He knows that London was once under the sea and there are shells embedded in the stones of Poplar Library. He knows where the plague pits and the bear-baiting dens used to be. He can point out where the Vikings thundered up the Thames in their longboats and where they got befuddled by the eddies and drifts at Bow Creek. He knows that the body of a whale was dug up out of the marsh at the West India. He's witnessed dogfights. He knows where to find bare-knuckle fighters or nancy boys.

Jane Fulcher's favourite story, one her father often tells, concerns two mastiffs and a cow. The cow had been left to graze on the marsh south of Poplar in the loop of the Thames. The dogs, whose job it was to protect the cow from hungry poachers, were chained to the animal's feet. Every week a marshman came along and left meat for the dogs and between times they dug for worms and pounced on any small thing that crossed their path. But a mist came down as mists often did in the marsh and the cow, wandering about and unable to see its feet, stumbled on its chains and fell into a nearby bog, catapulting its unfortunate protectors into the quicksand. After a struggle the cow sank into the slime and died but, being lighter, the dogs remained on the surface for a while longer. For four days and nights the residents of Poplar heard a terrible wailing, but were too frightened to go down to the bog and see what was afoot. Rumours rushed around that the devil had landed in the marsh and was taunting them before making his move. When the marshman eventually returned to check on his charge he found two mastiff heads preserved in the marshy brine, their jaws open as if in a long, last howl of injustice. And that is how, Frenchie says, the Isle of Dogs got its name.

The stories have a fearful power. Whenever his children are defiant, Frenchie threatens to abandon them on barges that will carry them out on the tide beyond Southend to the Black Deep where their bodies will be consumed by whales and sea snakes.

Whales and sea snakes, nippers, whales and sea snakes.

CHAPTER 2

Leonard Page's early childhood is a good deal sketchier than my grandmother's. It's a matter of gathering what facts there are.

Len was born in Corbets Tey, a hamlet ten miles north of the Thames in southwest Essex. Today, the place is an undifferentiated huddle of suburban housing perched on the shoulder of the London orbital motorway as it dips down to the Thames at the Dartford Crossing. The land is flat and scoured by the wind that pours into East Anglia from the Urals. Hedges of stunted elderflowers and crabs give some respite, but nothing is strong enough to contain the eastern blasts. The frost is often hard. On a particularly brisk morning you can wander around the copses, picking up the bodies of dunnocks and other small birds which have succumbed to the cold during the night. Most often the sky is obscured by shapeless cloud. You can go from one week to the next and not see the outline of the sun. It is good farming country though, the soil sodden and alkaline, perfect for brassicas and grain, and where there are still fields they are neatly ploughed, the soil blooming from powder fertilisers. A chemical smell mixes with the stench of petrol fumes from the ceaseless flow of traffic, but a hundred years ago, when my grandfather was born, Corbets Tey was as remote and peaceful a place as you could find.

In 1903, the year of Len's birth, Corbets was the smallest of the villages between the Ingrebourne River and the marshy edges of the Thames. To call it a village, even, is to grace it with a significance it did not have, for Corbets Tey was little more than a satellite of Upminster, which itself lay in the shadow of Romford, the nearest market town. You couldn't miss it, exactly, but you could pass through and imagine you were still in Upminster because the two villages were only a mile or so apart, though there was in fact a world between them. In 1849 a railtrack was built through Upminster and Ockenden but it bypassed Corbets Tey, and by the time my grandfather was born the place had stagnated. The first bus to pass through the village in 1924 caused such a stir that children were let out of school to watch it trundle by.

From Upminster, the Corbets road swung south, slinking between the flint walls of Gaines' Manor across a watercress stream from where it climbed a rare hill into Corbets itself. Just before the centre of the village, such as it was, the road bent east towards North Ockenden and a few paces further south there was a turning on the right, then called Green Lane. The lane meandered past Great Sunnings Farm to Sullens Farm from where it rejoined the Ockenden Road at a sharp bend known as Cabbage Corner. On either side of Cabbage Corner there were neat rows of workers' cottages, weatherboarded against the rushing wind, and it is probable that Len Page was born in one of these.

It would be comforting to imagine Len Page playing along the reedy streams and among the bean fields, or hunting pheasants in the woods, wood pigeons in the fields, perch in Ingrebourne River and rabbits everywhere, the sky stretched over him as soft as a petal, his lungs filled with damp air. But the fact of the matter is he probably spent much of his early life wading through mud. There was a great deal of that in the lowlands. From November to March there was little else but wind and mud and spells of bitter cold when the roads turned to brown ice.

The name Page conjures images of books and education, but the Pages had none of either. They were illiterate agricultural labourers who worked the land at Emery's Farm in North Upminster. Len's father, Jim, was a stern and silent man who passed his days among the dumb rows of cabbages. He was happier alone with his plough horses – Suffolk Punches and Percherons – than he was around people. He had no appetite for idle chatter or gossip and preferred to listen to what the breeze had to say. He was fond enough of his wife, Emily Nottage, but she didn't really interest him. After their marriage in 1895 he discovered that a woman's world was convoluted and women themselves hard to please, so he stopped trying. His children did not rouse him either. He and Emily had four: Thomas, Leonard, and twins Emily Maria (known as Ria) and Daisy. As a matter of duty he provided for them, but since he didn't own a farm to pass on to them they were incidentals in his life. It wasn't that he disliked them, just that he preferred his Percherons.

The Nottages were labourers, too. They worked at Blush Farm in Chafford Heath and at Hawthorn Farm in Upminster. Emily's father, Thomas Nottage, was as much a loner as her husband, and his wife, Jane, Emily's mother, had learned to put up with it. Thomas and Jane had six children: Alfred, William, Thomas, Emily, Walter and Fred. As soon as they were old enough to pick up a shovel, the boys joined their father labouring, leaving Jane and Emily responsible for the endless domestic chores as well as the kitchen garden and the chickens.

Things were not easy for the Nottage family. They moved around a great deal, Thomas never staying at one farm for more than a few years and the whole family having to up sticks and trundle their belongings to the next place. The children, Emily included, grew up to be independent-minded and with a sense of the impermanence of things.

By all accounts, my great grandmother Emily made a disgruntled countrywoman. She chafed against the solitude and routine. Country life held no mystique for Emily. In her view, clouds were no more interesting than buckets of water and fields of wheat were simply unmade bread. Emily longed for the glamour of the town. She complained that there was nothing to do in Corbets Tey but work. He restlessness rubbed the family raw. Whenever she could she would dress in her best and take herself off to Romford Market. The market had been the social and trade hub of southern Essex since at least the mid-thirteenth century. Farmers from all over the area gathered at The Blucher's Head in the market square to discuss the weather and the current state of their crops. On summer evenings men and women danced jigs together in the square. On May Day they ran around the May Pole, and that may well be how Jim and Emily first met.

On the opposite side of the square from The Blucher's Head stood The Windmill and Bells. The Windmill was rather downmarket, its clientele the poachers and the labourers who worked for the farmers. At The Windmill they would trade news of labouring opportunities and ferrets. Jim Page bought and sold his ferrets here and picked up poaching tips. Jim was a keen poacher and a generous teacher. As soon as they were old enough he taught his sons the art of setting traps and snares and hunting with dogs and ferrets, and from the age of ten or so the boys spent much of their spare time snaring rabbits and netting birds on the riverine marshes at Rainham, Wennington, Hornchurch and Aveley, or fishing for perch in Rainham Creek. It was illegal but the marshes were never much of a target for the law. Thomas and Len grew up with a poacher's contempt for authority and a sense too that a world of plenty existed outside the confines of their current circumstance and they had a right to go out and get their share.

They were desperately poor. In 1914 an agricultural labourer's pay of thirteen shillings a week was not enough to buy food for a large family, and when the weather was bad Jim took home as little as half that sum. They were always insecure. If a labouring man got caught under the thresher and smashed his leg, or the crop failed or the farmer bought a tractor, the labourer's family would be turned out of its tied cottage and left to fend for itself.

In 1914 the Agricultural and Rural Workers Union began organising strikes all over East Anglia, calling for a stable wage and more security of employ. The strikes went on for months and became bitter. Disgruntled labourers began burning fields and cutting cattle loose. George Lansbury, the socialist MP for Poplar, travelled to Essex in the hope of encouraging the strikers to carry on, but these were tiny, rural communities and the strikes split them down the middle. It was then that Jim Page finally made up his mind to leave. However much he loved the country, life there had become too hard and he was in no doubt that the tractor and threshing machine, the new American grain ships he'd heard talk of and the growth of trade from the colonies were going to make it harder for labourers like himself. He decided to pack up the family and put them on the train to London. It was only thirty miles to the west but it might as well have been thirty thousand.

In my family, East is where you start out and West is where you hope to end your days. For us, East has never been the east of the sunrise, of Eden or of new beginnings. East is nowhere glamorous or elemental or softly perfumed. The East we know is the east of the Anglian Marshes and the east of the East End of London. East is grimy city terraces in fog-plagued streets. East is biting winds and soggy ground and a dying livelihood.

A wagon pulled by a Percheron takes the Page family from their flinty home in Green Lane to the train station at Upminster. Their few things – a couple of blankets, sheets, a rabbit fur cover and the bits and bobs of Emily's trousseau – are slung in the back between hay bales. As they round Cabbage Corner, Jim inspects the familiar, loved terrain, his face dimming with tears, while Emily smiles ahead and the children play catch-what-can in the back. At the station they unpack the bags, pat the Percheron goodbye and stand on the platform watching the empty space along the track until, finally, when their eyes are growing sore from looking, the first intimations of smoke come into view, followed by the maroon carriages and the great green-panelled engine of the train itself.

Oh look Da, says Len Page, only eleven then, and curious. It's got 'Upminster' painted on the side. That's the name of the train, ain't it?

Machines ain't given names. Jim shakes his head at his son's foolishness. Only livin' things are given names. So that can't be the name thar, see? That's only where it's from.

Then the cloud of smoke rises, obscuring, for an instant, the family standing on the platform edge, and they heave their bags into the carriage and take their places on the hard wooden seats and the train begins to haul itself slowly westwards towards Upminster and Romford and on to London. From the seat beside the window Len Page watches the landscape of his childhood receding behind them. Then, feeling exploratory, he gets up and takes himself off along the aisle to the next carriage, where a fat man with a goitre is sitting reading a newspaper. He edges along the aisle and for a moment the combined swaying of the train and smell of coal smoke overtakes him and he does not notice a man in uniform bowling along the aisle towards him.

You going somewhere, son?

No, he says.

Well get back to your seat, then, sonny boy.

He follows Len to the carriage door.

Hey mister, says Len, remembering the conversation with his father, what's this engine called?

This? The man in the uniform smiles. This is the Upminster, son. The number twenty-one.

Thank you mister.

The man in uniform ruffles Len's dun brown hair.

You interested in trains, sonny?

No.

Ah, says the man, darkening. You get back to your place then.

Sliding on to the wooden bench, Len tries not to catch his father's eye. He is glad when the Upminster begins to draw into Fenchurch Street on the eastern side of the City of London and with its brakes squealing and the smoke pouring from its funnel finally slows to a halt in the wide iron arms of the station.

The journey from Upminster to London takes just under an hour but this is the first time that Jim Page or Emily Nottage or their children have ever made it. They hire a hackney carriage to take them east from Fenchurch Street. 'As far as I could see were the solid walls of brick, the slimy pavements and the screaming streets,' Jack London wrote in 1904, and the scene isn't so different ten years later. The carriage takes them through the sullen alleyways and lanes of Aldgate and Whitechapel and out to the market stalls at the Mile End Waste which dot the road as far as the eye can see like a set of ragged flags. On either side there are more people than they have ever imagined could live in one place, even such a place as London.

The Thames pushes east towards the sea, but the city's wealth has for centuries drifted westwards, against the direction of the prevailing winds, to escape what Sir William Petty described four hundred years ago as the 'fumes, steams and stinks of the whole easterly pile'. The booty of the docks flowed west too, along the wide East London arterials – Mile End Road, East India Dock Road, Commercial Road, West India Dock Road, Roman Road, Royal Victoria Dock Road – to more prosperous parts of London where people lived luckier lives.

You move to the East End if you are desperate, and the Pages are. There is unskilled work to be had in the factories, in the finishing trades and around the docks, and a man with strong hands and an eager face can just about scrape by and, more to the point, feel that he is among those who understand as well as he does the predicaments of exile. Over the centuries, all Europe's diasporas have met here: first Huguenots, men and women like the Fulchers, then Jews fleeing Russian pogroms, Irish on the lam from the potato famine, and after them Armenians, Lithuanians, Poles, more Jews and other refugees from religious persecutions, and finally families like the Pages, the English rural poor. A hundred years on it is the same, though the mix has changed. Wander through any of the East End's markets on a sunny afternoon and you will pass by Somalis, Polynesians, Vietnamese, Cambodians, Liberians, Eritreans, Indonesians, East African Asians; most of whom are there because they were obliged to leave somewhere else. The Pages are just one point on a continuum stretching across the centuries.

So they settle in East Ham, which is then a small suburb of 'respectable' working class homes beside the fastest-growing, poorest, most overcrowded and most heavily industrialised area in London. Emily has family in East Ham and for a while they are able to rent a room from them; six people, taking turns on the bed and with the sounds of another family leaking through the walls. Things are not as bad as they might be. Jim soon finds work as a labourer in a lumber yard and before many months have passed, they have a little money. Emily likes not having to travel to market. There are stalls and shops on every street corner. Jim takes comfort in small things. On his way to work every morning, he passes fields. Occasionally cows wander along their modest, tree-lined street and once in a while, if he closes his eyes, he can almost imagine he is back in Corbets Tey.

CHAPTER 3

In the years before the first war, the Fulcher family concerns are the concerns of respectability – nits, bedbugs and the price of marg. They're not on the rise, exactly, but they're not on the fall either, and there is a pleasing steadiness to life. Frenchie is bringing home most of his carpenter's wage and Sarah is able to top it up with the few shillings she makes from taking in the mending for James Looke's laundry in Ullin Street. Not so far away, not so far at all, there are families whose children go about barefoot and shit in pits in the cellar; families whose lives are reduced to a matter of other people's pockets and what might be in them; families who might go under altogether if it weren't for Sally Army soup. Not the Fulchers. The Fulchers all have boots (with cardboard soles fitted periodically by Frenchie), and each is in possession of his or her own outer garment. The Fulcher children only have nits when they catch them from other children, and there is bread and marg at every mealtime. No Fulcher child has ever had to dip for a living, and not a drop of Sally Army soup has passed Fulcher lips.

Not all the families in Ullin Street are so lucky. Among these are the Jorrocks who live at number twelve. Matty and Tom Jorrocks have to collect the horse shit off the roads to sell to the families with vegetable plots, and their mother Mary has been seen standing in the soup kitchen queue. Matty and Tom have boots, though they are taken from different pairs and Matty's toes explode from his. Between them they share a ragged twill which they take it in turns to wear, Matty every morning on the way school and Tom on the way back. Their destinies are already set. At the age of fourteen they will leave school and if they are lucky they'll find work in the docks, the factories or the sweatshops. Others will take their emptied places and so it will go on.

All the children of school age living in Ullin Street are obliged to attend the same school, just a few roads away in Bright Street. The Bright Street School is a hulking, optimistic construction of red brick sandwiched between a terrace of houses and a forest of pubs, within whose damp walls the children of East Poplar are daily expected, by some mysterious means, to obtain an education.

Mathematics: three times six is eighteen.

Religion: the Seven Deadly Sins: greed, lust, gluttony, covetousness, etc.

History: the Tudor monarchs: Haitch, He and Me. That's Henry VII, Henry VIII, Edward V, Mary I and Elizabeth I.

Politics: the sun never sets on the British Empire.

At eight o'clock every morning the doors of Ullin Street open and the children tumble out and make their way towards Bright Street. It is no more than a five-minute walk but for the Fulcher children it is the longest five minutes of their day because Matty and Tom Jorrocks have made it their young lives' work to torment the Fulchers. The only Fulcher Tom and Matty never tease is Rosie and that is because Rosie is thirteen and pretty.

Plain Jane. Plain Janey Foolshit, shout Matty and Tom at the gaggle of miserable Fulchers. Mouldy Maudie Foolshit, Johnny Pongy Bastard-Foolshit.

Sometimes a stone will soar into the air and land thump on the back of one of the Fulcher children. Once, a dead rat comes at them. Another time a clump of horse shit. Banned by Sarah from talking to the Jorrocks, the Fulcher children have little choice but to carry on along Ullin Street, but nothing seems to discourage Tom and Matty.

Foolshit. Plainey Janey.

Mum, why do they call us names? asks Jane.

Because they're common.

Why? says Jane.

Her mother smiles at her girl and winks and shakes her head.

Blimey, the questions you ask! C'm 'ere and drink your tea.

Jane is an average student in every lesson with the exception of writing. Twice a day a single slate comes around the class and the children are expected to inscribe on to it whatever the teacher demands. However hard Jane toils over the slate, her right hand will not write. The left produces perfect scrolls, beautiful lines and slashes but the right is like a wayward child. Very often she can get nothing from it but squiggles and odd little polka dots.

Only witches and imbeciles write with their left hands, Jane Fulcher, says Miss Whiting, the teacher. Which are you? Now, right hand, please. What are you waiting for?

I can't do it, Miss.

A long sigh, eyes raising to the roof. How old are you, Jane?

Ten, Miss.

And you still can't write your own name? What does that mean, Jane Fulcher?

I don't know, Miss.

It means you are insubordinate and lazy, Jane Fulcher.

Righty-ho, Miss.

Miss Whiting sweeps from her desk clutching a ruler and, rushing forwards, brings it down on the knuckles of Jane Fulcher's left hand. Sometimes she will use a buckled belt or a shoe. Every now and then Miss Whiting will add in the backs of Jane's knees and elbows for good measure, reciting her indictments with each blow. Insubordinate. Whack. Lazy. Whack. At the age of ten, Jane's left hand is a five-fingered callus, the right a ghost afraid of its own shadow. The right-handed children break into titters of relief and contempt. They fear the hand impairment is contagious. Whenever Jane goes near them they tend to peel away.

When they arrive home of an evening Rosie will say, Never mind, Janey, I love yer, and Jane will feel better for a while, even though she knows that Rosie can afford to be nice because she is pretty.

Janey got done in writing class again today, Rosie will tell their mother, fetching some salted water to bathe the stinging hand.

I never needed no writing nor nothing and it never bothered me, Sarah will say, and giving her daughter's hands a little kiss she will wrap them in a pair of old mittens so that Frenchie won't be bothered by the sight of them.

To avoid Matty and Tom, the Fulchers begin taking a different route to school, one that puts them in the way of the confectionery store of Mrs Selina Folkman on Zetland Street. To Jane, the store is a sugar palace. In the window are bricks of pink and white coconut ice sitting on a paving of cream fudge with cherry-spotted nougat arches.

Get a move on, Janey, you can't have none, says Rosie, each time Jane's footfall slows as she reaches Selina Folkman's store. But it's no good. Within days, Jane can think of nothing else. Bit by bit the sugar palace consumes her. Rowntree's Treacle Toffee, Fry's Chocolate Crème, McIntyre's Toffee Tablet, Maynards Rum 'n' Raisin. In her mind the names become exotic friends. Mr Treacle Toffee, stern and rather bitter; Miss Crème, delicate, soft and yielding; Mrs Rum 'n' Raisin, sweet and old and as drunk as Mrs Jorrocks. Her confectionery characters take up residence in Jane's heart.

On the first Friday of every month Frenchie comes home with a twist of brown paper bought from an Indian toffee seller who stands on a busy crossroads on Frenchie's way home.

Who's after a bit of toffee? cries Frenchie.

Me! Me!

The children cram around.

Only a penny's worth mind, says Frenchie, and you'll have to work for it. Righty-ho, name four ships, says Frenchie.

Patonga, Port Vindex . . . The words roll around the children's mouths.

His Majesty's, says John.

Uruguay Star, Leeds City . . .

Frenchie fetches the stub of a cigarette from behind his ear, lights it and leans back luxuriantly, the smoke playing in curls around his face, while his children throw anxious glances at one another, the fruit box table, their mother.

I don't know why you have to put them through it, says Sarah.

If you don't know the names of things, how you gonna call on nothing? Frenchie says.

Sarah stares at him and shrugs, returning to her mending while the children sit bolt upright on the bed, imagining the feel of the toffee, the smell, the long, sensuous melt. Their father draws again on his stub.

What kind of name is His Majesty's anyway?

It ain't a name at all, says Rosie.

Correct, says Frenchie reaching for the twist of brown paper in his pocket.

And what do they make from tin, Janey?

Tins? says Jane.

Voila! says Frenchie. Now, who'll be having a bit . . . ?

Just after Jane turns eleven, a dirty-skinned, yellow-haired girl appears in Miss Whiting's class. In itself, this isn't much of an event. Children come and go. A bitter winter is enough to take off one or two. All the same, there is something about this particular girl which attracts Jane. Perhaps it is her confidence, the sure set of her jaw. Perhaps it is the faint smell of violets she gives off, recalling violet crèmes and violet dragees and violet lozenges. Perhaps it is the vague sense of familiarity. Perhaps it is a thousand things. All Jane knows is that it *is*.

The yellow-haired girl senses this too and at the end of the second day she is waiting for Jane at the school gates.

Who's this then? Rosie asks.

Guess, says the yellow-haired girl.

Can't, won't and shan't, says Rosie, pulling her sister out into the street.

The yellow-haired girl follows them across Bright Street and out into St Leonard's Road, singing in a jangly voice: Poplar is popular but Wapping is topping.

At the crossroads Jane turns and says, So, why pick on us to tell?

Pretty soon the party reaches Ullin Street and there, ahead of them, standing beside the alley that runs along the church, are Matty and Tom, gazing at something lying in the mud.

What you got then? asks the yellow-haired girl.

The matted body of a black and white cat looms from the shadows, still alive but with the legs splayed at unnatural angles. The eyes are out and its mouth oozes blood mixed with an ill-looking foam.

We din do the eyes, says Tom. They was done already.

There is a moment's pause while all parties take this in.

Wanna look? asks Tom. At that moment the creature lifts its head and slowly begins to drag itself towards the deepness of the alley.

That's disgusting, says the yellow-haired girl.

Gis a penny or we'll stamp on it, says Matty.

Drop dead, says the yellow-haired girl. Matty Jorrocks raises his boot and grins.

The poor thing, says the yellow-haired girl and, reaching for a broken piece of brick on the pavement, she darts in front of the Jorrocks boys and brings the brick down hard on the creature's head.

There, she says, brushing the brick dust from her hands as Tom and Matty tumble down the street. Jane and the yellow-haired girl find themselves alone above the body of the cat, each taking the measure of the other.

How's about we play ginger? says the girl.

In ginger you tie the one doorknob to its neighbour, ring the doorbells and speed off to the nearest vantage.

My mum says ginger is common, says Jane, sensing a surge of bad feeling running through her belly.

Please yerself, says the girl, drawing herself up, the yellow hair falling across her face like sunlight. I don't care anyway.

And that, over the years, is what Jane Fulcher finds most thrilling about her friend Dora Trelling. Dora Trelling really doesn't care.

Jane begins meeting Dora after school. They walk together to Mrs Folkman's emporium on Zetland Street and discuss the relative merits of sweets they have never tasted.

Cough candy, now, there's a nice little tablet, says Jane.

They fall silent for a moment, imagining the crust of sugar on the outside, the damp, welcoming interior.

Dor, wha's your all-time favourite sweet?

They scan the rainbow piles in the shop window.

I ain't never had none of 'em. Wha's yours?

Lemme see, says Jane, running her mind across imaginary tastes.

Liquorice comfits or montelimar? Fruit gems or marshmallow? Tell the truth, Dor, I'm a little bit partial to the lot but all considered, I think montelimar gets it.

Liar, liar, says Dora. Liar, liar, pants on fire.

CHAPTER 4

On a hot June day, just before the war, and sensing their lives are about to change, the Fulchers take a trip, their first, to the Royal Victoria Gardens on the riverbank between Silvertown and North Woolwich. Dressed in their Sunday best (which is also their Sunday worst and their Monday best), they make their way across the Lea Bridge where they stop for a while to admire Frenchie's boats at Orchard Place. They are not technically Frenchie's boats, of course, but it was Frenchie who laid their decks and Frenchie who panelled their cockpits and Frenchie has names for all of them.

There's the Rosetta, nippers, ain't she a beauty? And the Edie down there, a lovely slender little ship. Beyond it in the grey coat, the Maudie. Ah me boats, me boats.

Where's the Janey, Da?

Oh the Janey. Frenchie rubs a hand over his hair and shakes his head. Well, I don't know as there is a Janey yet, poppet. Not yet.

They wander over the bridge into Canning Town. The younger children, Artie and Edie, are joyful and pestering. Can they have an ice cream, a gobstopper, a penny bag of Indian toffee? The elder four, Rosie, Frances Maud, John and Jane, drag their heels a little, as if by walking more slowly they might keep the day going on for ever.

Opened in 1851 for those who could not afford the Great Exhib-
ition, the Gardens are one of the few spots of green between the
docks and the Thames and the only place to the east of the Lea,
aside from Lyle Park, where there is an unimpeded view of the
river water. Despite their reputation for being unsafe and swampy,
the Gardens were generally crowded with women and children
marking time while their men drank in the vast dockers' pubs on
the North Woolwich Road. Decades ago they had been famous for
staging Monster Baby shows, where babies with swollen, scarlet
heads, or three hands, or rows of nipples like pigs, were displayed
for the edification of paying onlookers. The monster babies had long
since gone when the Fulchers arrived, replaced by the fortune-tellers,
jugglers and cardmen, but the Gardens still had a sinister reputation
and there were rumours that they were haunted after dark by the
souls of those who drowned nearby when the Princess Alice went
down at Gallions Reach thirty years before.

Each spring and summer throughout the late 1860s and early
1870s, the Princess Alice, a steam-driven pleasure boat, had ferried
city-worn families to the pleasure gardens at Rosherville and
Gravesend, stopping off at the Royal Victoria Gardens to pick up
passengers on its journey eastwards. On a Tuesday in September
1878, at about teatime, the Alice left Sheerness as usual. Just after
dusk the boat approached Tripcocks Point, at the northernmost crick
of Gallions Reach. It was only as she turned the point that George
Long, the Alice's first mate, spotted the Bywell Castle, an 890-ton
collier ship bound for Newcastle, heading towards them at speed
and only 150 yards distant. There was nothing to be done but wait
for the impact.

Within four minutes, seven hundred and fifty men, women and
children were in the water just east of the Gardens' jetty and almost
directly on the spot where the Northern Outfall Sewer opened to

discharge north London's sewage into the Thames. It was only a few yards to shore but the Thames is fast at Gallions Reach and the sewage poisoned those desperately trying to reach land. Within twenty minutes, six hundred and fifty men, women and children had drowned, their soiled bodies drifting in at the Victoria Gardens. They were buried in Woolwich Old Cemetery but it was said that their ghosts still inhabited the waters at Gallions Reach and cast curses and spells on Silvertown and all those who had failed to save them.

The Fulchers aren't thinking about the Alice on this day. They are too busy considering where they might eat the picnic they have brought and whether they will have ice creams or shrimps from one of the food stands afterwards. Finding an empty bench beside the rose garden (Sarah and Jane are especially fond of roses) the children settle themselves around their parents and fall on fish paste sand-wiches made from yesterday's bread and a bit of drip mixed in. They wash them down with cold, black, sweet tea from an old beer bottle with a ground glass top while Frenchie spins yarns about the baby monsters he remembers as a small child and how for months afterwards he would check himself on waking to make sure he hadn't become one of them during the night. And when the business of eating is done, the girls skip off to inspect a crimson parrot tied to a post which bobs up and down and croaks 'Daisy, Daisy' in exchange for a penny, and the boys join the crowd gathering for a demon-stration of a fire pump given by two smiling London firemen.

On their return Frenchie buys them all an ice cream from Dela-mura's ice cart and they wander down to the river and wave at the pleasure boats passing by with the ice cream melting down their chins. Frenchie lifts the youngest two on to the Woolwich Free Ferry to gawp at the pauper children shouting 'throw out your mouldies' to the passengers on the steamers tied up at Woolwich

Pier. They watch the scattering of coins from ship to shore, while Rosie, Frances Maud and Jane feed the pigeons on the pier.

The afternoon is hazy, the sun emerging every so often to flood the Gardens with its polished light. The youngest Fulcher children play hide and seek and grandmothers' footsteps between the trees while their father smokes on a park bench by the river and reads his paper. Their mother dozes and the older children watch the passage of ships along the river, trying to guess their names. Then, much too soon, the sun begins to take cover behind the afternoon clouds and Frenchie Fulcher rises to signal it is time to start the long walk back home.

And that is the last really happy day any of them can remember. By the autumn the Great War has begun and by October the first German bomb has fallen on London.

A stifling afternoon in early September 1914 finds Jane Fulcher and Dora Trelling hiding behind a postbox on the East India Dock Road while several thousand men in uniform thump along the granite in the direction of the ships that will take them off to war. It is rather overwhelming, this column of marching men, and rather thrilling too, to two young girls who have never ventured from their birthplace and who cannot know what any war − let alone this one − will bring. All along the route, men and women are leaning from windows laced with bunting, waving and whistling. There's a band playing rousing military tunes and everywhere people are fluttering little Union Jacks on sticks and clapping. A few, women mostly, are hurrying alongside the marchers, delaying the moment when their husband or brother or son will finally slip from sight. One or two are crying, but only one or two, because the papers say it will be the shortest of wars and how could anyone who has witnessed the ineluctable power of the great British Empire think otherwise.

Me dad says signing up is for the birds, says Dora.

The men continue to march by, their faces sombre and set in patterns suggestive of faraway thoughts.

D'you think they'll be getting theirselfs killed, Dor? asks Jane.

Nah, no chance. It's the Germs what's getting theirselfs killed.

Dor, says Jane, you got some coinage on yer?

Dora shakes her head.

Nothing. Why?

Every week they go through the same routine. The answer is always the same. Jess thinkin 'bout sweets, is all.

They peer out from behind the postbox at the khaki-coloured column in the road.

When we win the war, do you think we'll have more money, Dor?

Sure as eggs is eggs, Janey pet.

They make their way south then east to Bow Lane and find themselves in a small crowd outside number 278 – William Utz the butcher's. This crowd is quite unlike the one waving on the soldiers. There is something ugly about it. One of them, a young man with a reddened face, has grabbed a brick and is looking as though he means to throw it at Utz's shop window. Some of the crowd appear to be egging him on; others are standing back, shaking their heads.

What's goin on, Dor? says Jane.

Don't ask me, Janey girl.

I suppose he ain't paid the tallyman.

I suppose that's it, Janey.

The two girls pass through the crowd and out the other side, but the air has changed, as though a high wind had moved through the Poplar they knew and set everything at an unfamiliar angle.

Jane doesn't mention the incident at home, partly because she doesn't know what to say about it and partly – and this is the puzzling bit – because she feels somehow responsible. She hopes the thing – whatever it is – will go away, and for a few hours it does, until at tea that day when Sarah puts a glistening slab of headcheese on the table next to the customary bread and jam and marg.

I got it at Utz's place, explains Sarah, settling herself on the bed next to her children. A chap was selling everythin' off cheap right out at the front. He had a little trestle going there, with Utz's meat piled up, bits of glass all over everything but nuffink you couldn't pick out. I dunno where Utz was but when things is going off cheap you don't ask questions.

The family stares at the headcheese sitting on the plate, glowing in pink loveliness, with its little jewels of brain, ear, cheek and snout meat. How long is it since they had meat of any kind? None of them can remember. Since the start of the war, everything has become so expensive.

I ain't gonna eat no Hun meat, Frenchie says. Not now.

Silence falls. The children bite their lips and stare at their laps.

Me neither, says John eventually, sliding away from the table.

Nor me, says Frances Maud.

And that is when Jane notices Frenchie's eyes on her. Now she is sure that the whole business at Utz's is her fault.

Sarah gets up from the bed and moves the headcheese over to her side of the table.

Oh you are silly billies. Go on, Edie, you take some, pet.

Edie shoots her mother a look then shakes her head. Me and Artie are going out to play now, she says, dragging her little brother out of the room and down the stairs.

Frenchie gets up from the table, goes to his chair by the fire and lights a cigarette and now there are only two people left sitting beside the table with the slab. Silly billies, repeats Sarah, slicing the slab in two. Here you go, Janey.

Jane sits there for a moment, thinking about the boy with the brick and the ugly words spilling from the crowd, and every part of her is saying no except the part that counts, and suddenly she can hear the headcheese saying, *I know how badly you want me, Janey*, and then it's too late and her tongue is lapping around the jellied crust and her teeth are sinking into the pillow of blushing flesh.

Later, when she and Sarah are down at the yard tap washing the jam jars, and the headcheese is making grunting noises in her stomach, Jane says, How big is the war, Mum?

It's the size of the world, pet, her mother says, poking at some greasy mark.

Does that mean it's going on in Aldgate and Whitechapel?

Course it do!

Is the war going on in the Empire then?

Sarah Fulcher shakes the water off her hands. The concrete of the back yard is thick with city heat. It is too hot to work, too hot to think much. Even Bobs has excused himself from his ratting duties and is lying in the coolest corner of the yard, panting.

I wouldn't know nothing about that, Janey dear, sighs Sarah, rubbing her moonish face with the damp on her hands.

Mum? says Jane.

Her mother sighs and tightens her lips.

Oh, you're a right little Miss Why this evening. What is it now?

Don't the sun never set on the war then?

They make their way up the stairs, avoiding the gaps in the banisters where someone has broken pieces off for firewood. Their room still smells faintly of the headcheese.

Well now, I don't suppose it ever do, says Sarah.

Jane rescues a few hairs escaping from her plait. The war is a puzzle to her. If Britain rules the waves, then what is there to fight about? Why is Mr Utz bad now? They've been buying tripe off him for years and he wasn't bad then. Has the badness got something to do with the brawn or has it got more to do with Utz himself, with the very name Utz maybe?

Mum, we ain't foreigners, are we?

Janey, how can we be foreigners? Sarah returns to her sewing for a moment but Jane's brow is so furrowed and her face so perplexed that even her mother, the most unobservant of women, is driven to wonder what kind of storm is collecting in the girl's mind.

Ah I see, Sarah says, her lips squeezed round pins. Yer thinking about how yer dad come to be known as Frenchie, ain't yer? French ain't foreign, love. It's on the same side as us, innit? Ask yer father when he comes home from the pub and he'll tell yer.

She glances at her daughter momentarily.

Probly give yer a good clumping, though, an all.

There were anti-German protests all over the East End that week. In some parts things got so bad that traders with German-sounding names put up boards outside their shops saying 'Lewis Hermann is English' and the like, but still it went on. Utz returned but was run out of his shop; in Silvertown boys threw bottles at the houses of German glass blowers and there was much discussion about whether the Lithuanians who lived in the same street were really only Germans by another name. And then, after a few days, the whole thing blew over, because when it came down to it there were a great many foreigners in the East End and you couldn't throw bottles at everyone, and in any case it would be a waste of the deposit on the bottles.

To Jane, the Great War had begun as an enigma and it stayed

that way. On her way to the market she'd see women streaming
from the munitions factories with faces yellow from picric acid, the
local boys running after them shouting 'Chinkie Chinkie Chinkie'.
Policemen rode around the streets of Poplar on new bicycles with
sandwich boards over their chests reading AIR RAID, TAKE COVER,
but no one ever did because they were more interested in gawping
at the bicycles. In the winter of 1917 she was woken by a dreadful
thunder, throatier than any bomb and deeper than the sound of
shelling. The sky went red, then green and the smell of burning
flour came over. The Brunner Mond Munitions plant at Silvertown
had blown itself to bits and taken half of Silvertown with it. Afterwards, she discovered that the blast had hurled metal across the
Thames into East Greenwich, where it had ripped apart a gasholder
and sent a blue flame jetting fifty feet into the sky. She recalled how
odd it was that this news had left her cold and unmoved, with
neither fear nor anticipation. Other memories had no particular
feelings attached to them but remained with her all the same. She
remembered a man slumped in the doorway of a pub, blood snaking
down his chin. She remembered men returning from the front, their
eyes and legs and arms bandaged and their faces closed. She recalled
seeing an enemy aeroplane which had been at the People's Palace
in Mile End. But somehow these were abstract things.

The winter of 1915 is bitter cold, there never seems to be enough
coal dust to keep dry and warm, and day after day the inhabitants
of Poplar have to go about their lives in clammy undergarments
with their socks half-frozen between their toes. Frenchie is working
all hours at the boat yard. One particularly frosty day he is fitting out
a barge with his docker's neckerchief at his throat and his cap wedged
down over his head and a cigarette bobbing up and down between
his lips when a rattle starts up in his lungs. By seven o'clock his
breath is as heavy as rock. All night Sarah simmers onions in milk

and holds the warm halves to her husband's chest but by morning he is worse, and his breath is like broken bellows and the children are afraid and begin to harbour a secret hope that by the time they come home from school he will have disappeared. Still, he insists on trudging to work, but just before midday a clerk's assistant brings him back, staggering and incoherent. He ain't no use, the clerk says. Had to carry 'im 'ere almost. Sarah makes sugared tea and puts her husband to bed, still wearing his neckerchief and protesting his fitness, but halfway through the night he wakes up afraid.

Jesus, Mary and Joseph, not this, he cries. What'll become?

Shh, says Sarah. You'll be right as rain in a jiffy-jiff-jiff.

But Frenchie doesn't get better in a jiffy-jiff, or anything like. When his foreman pays a visit to the house at Ullin Street three days later, Frenchie Fulcher is worse, the breath lathing off his lungs and his nightsweats so torrid that you can smell them from outside the room. His eyes are red bowls, his skin the colour of custard. When he coughs, greyish sputum veined with blood oozes from the corners of his lips.

He's awful watery, says Sarah.

The foreman says it's more like pneumonia and advises Sarah to call a doctor, though he already knows a doctor will not be called.

Never mind, Mrs F, he says, patting the soft wodge of Sarah's arm. Don't you worry 'bout nothing, there'll be work in plenty waiting for Frenchie the moment he's well enough to do it. We got a war on, after all, ain't we?

A week drifts by, then another, and Frenchie's nightsweats begin to lose their putrid smell and dry up, and instead of the bloody sputum, great green gobbets of mucus appear whenever Frenchie coughs. From then on he is a little better every day but it is a long recuperation, marked by downturns and surging fevers.

Ah, Frenchie, you're a credit to us all, the foreman says when he next visits. Sure as eggs is eggs you'll be up and at it in no time and there'll be plenty of work 'cetra 'cetra.

Seeing the foreman to the door, Sarah braces herself and says, Listen, mister, we've had to do a spot of belt-tightening. I don't suppose . . . ?

Ah yes, says the foreman, shaking his head. Belts tightening all over the East End. Can almost hear 'em creak. I'm sorry, Mrs F, I really am. But belts is a family's business and none of mine.

For a week they live on the tuppences Sarah has put in a jam jar for Christmas. A cousin sends round soup and the odd half-loaf, a neighbour takes in the washing and Tarbun the grocer and Harwood the greengrocer are good enough to ease the Fulcher's credit. But once a poor family in the East End is taken with illness or unemployment there is no backstop that can prevent their fall, no neighbour or relative who can do more than slow its pace a little. The Fulchers are reduced to soup and bread scraped with lard, until the soup and the lard run out and then it's just bread. Hearing of their distress, the vicar's wife brings round porridge and, hovering over the bed where Frenchie is heaving, says, So I'll be seeing you in church, then? And Sarah replies, Right enough, Missus, but after the vicar's wife has left there is nothing she can do to persuade her husband.

Sarah, old girl, I ain't never been righteous and I ain't gonna start pretending now. Mebbe I'd be moved to do a spot of praising if the vicar's wife had turned up with pasties instead of porridge.

For a month the children go hungry every day. Their insides rumble through their lessons. In the evenings Sarah mops their tears and feeds them stale bread made soft in sugared water, but the sight and sound and smell and memory of food plague their waking moments and their dreams. The whole family is set to work. John junior brings in six shillings a week loading wagons at the coal yard, Frances Maud and Rosie find jobs in a munitions factory. The younger children run errands, mind horses and stand beside the queues for the music hall in Mile End Road fetching ices and beigels for those that want them. All the same, they live in a twilight of hunger. At night they hang around the dustbins at the back of Harwoods watching the pauper children rummaging for remains.

We'll never be like that will we, Rosie? asks Jane.

Never.

Because we're respectable, ain't we?

Because we are.

Their mother, who knows nothing of their night-time excursions, says, We ain't reduced just yet. Ee'll be as right as rain in no time and the foreman says there'll be more work for 'im than a man can do in a month of Sundays.

Six weeks after his first attack, Frenchie Fulcher wakes up one morning without a temperature. He feels his lungs, coughs experimentally and rises from the bed. Then he shaves, puts on his jacket and goes down to Orchard House. Calling for the foreman from the gate he shares a cup of tea with the guard there. He waits ten minutes, half an hour, an hour, two. After four hours the guard takes him to one side and says, The foreman ain't coming, sonny boy, now why don't you go home?

For the next eight months Frenchie does whatever he can, shouldering sacks for coalmen, heaving barrels off the brewers' drays, lugging carcasses at the abattoir, sorting cow bones for glue, but the work is lowly and piece-rate and Frenchie can't go at it as he might have done before his illness. His lungs still feel rackety and sometimes it's a terrible trouble just to catch a breath. At night they sit in the cold and dark, with no coals and no money for the gas lamp, their stomachs burning empty. In the space of a year their world fades to grey. Frenchie grows bitter. He misses his friends at Orchard House; he misses his small luxuries – his *Daily Mirror* and his smoke. Most of all he misses the life of a craftsman, a man with a skill to bring to the world. His heart boils and rages. He begins to spend more time in the company of a tuppeny pint at The Wellington Arms than with his family.

It ain't your father's fault, says Sarah. Ee's from carriage people, but blow me if the carriage ain't rolled clean away.

To keep her children warm when winter comes round again, Sarah smears their chests in goose grease and sews them into brown paper like jars of potted meat. The thought of losing another of her babies keeps her up nights and makes her hair go grey. They look so tired, now, and thin. At Christmas that year, 1916, the vicar's wife brings round a jug of soup with a piece of pig belly in it but Frenchie sends it back saying, She ain't buying us a place in heaven, we'll get there on our own. And so Christmas dinner that year is a plate of larded boiled potatoes and cabbage mush.

On New Year's Day they wake to the hollow horns of the ships in the West India.

What do you think they'll be cargoing? asks Jane.

Scrag of lamb and sugar pie, says Rosie.

Walnuts and marzipan, says Frances Maud.

Stuffed hearts and candied peel.

Faggots and mashed 'tater.

Bacon pudding with fruit junket.

Watch out, says Rosie, I'm gonna be sick.

The day turns cold and then gets colder. By night-time the ice has crept along the window panes and gathered in great ranges across the walls of the rooms. They go to bed struggling with their freezing breath. In the small hours, Rosie really is sick; by the morning she cannot eat or drink and her skin is as hot as coals.

She's watery, says Sarah, mopping her girl. But it isn't enough. Rosie begins to leak like a piece of bad piping. By the afternoon she's shaking so hard it's a wonder she doesn't shatter. Red spots have come up and she's moaning from the terrible pain in her stomach.

Woolwich Free Ferry's the thing, volunteers Mrs Smiley downstairs. Engine room warm as toast, don't cost you nothing and the captain lets the women with their sick 'uns ride all day.

There's an idea, says Sarah, but a kind of fatalism has set in and she does not take Rosie to ride the Woolwich Free Ferry. Most likely it would have made no difference anyway. After school that day, Sarah sends the children to a cousin, except Jane who will not leave Rosie.

The following night Frenchie goes out to fetch a doctor.

The doctor shakes his head.

Watery, see, says Sarah.

Typhoid is my guess. Doesn't help that she's so thin. Got malnutrition too most like.

Her parents gaze at their girl, the beautiful Rosetta, green skinned and dull-eyed but still beautiful in her going. Little Rosie.

Ah no, not this one, says Sarah. She reaches out for Frenchie's hand. It's always the good-looking ones.

The doctor is not unsympathetic but he has seen it a hundred times. He is hoping it will all end quickly so that he can sign the death certificate and get back to bed in time to catch a few more hours' sleep before dawn brings the next round. But Rosie hangs on another three days. Three torturing days and nights with Jane, sitting beside her sister on the bed, listening to the sound of her failing breath, smelling the musty odour of her sweats and telling her stories of Miss Crème and Mr Toffee and all the other inhabitants of Mrs Selina Folkman's.

CHAPTER 5

In 1917, the year of the Silvertown explosion, Jane leaves Bright Street School for good. Through a cousin of Dora's she hears there are vacancies for seamstresses at Moses' outfitters in Stepney, just east of the Mile End Waste, and a few days later Jane and Dora find themselves in front of an old brick house propped up with a makeshift scaffold made from telegraph poles and a peeling sign reading M. Moses, Quality Tailoring. Pushing through the entrance, they clamber up broken stairs into a shabby hallway and knock tentatively at a damp brown door marked Office. The supervisor, a grey-faced man in his fifties with a voice like an old hinge, confirms that their information is correct and that yes, indeed, Mr Moses is thinking of taking on a couple of youngsters. Moses prefers boys, whom he can apprentice, but there seems little point in taking on anyone who might be drafted in a year or two's time should the war go on that long. So, girls it is, says the supervisor, if girls it has to be. They can come back and speak to the proprietor himself on Friday afternoon when Mr Moses is always in the office sorting out the week's wages.

'Ere, Dor, says Jane, on the walk back to Poplar. D'you reckon Mr Moses is a Jew-Boy?

Not much! says Dora. Clot! What else'd he be? They make their way down to Commercial Road, past the alleys of Stepney. Me dad says all the Jew-Boys will end up in the poorhouse in the finish.

Not us, though.

Ah no, Janey, pet. Well we ain't common, see?

We're respectable, Dor.

We is that, Janey. We is that an' all.

Respectability takes up a great deal of Jane Fulcher's time. How to be it, how to show it, how to live it and how to keep on living it. The fact that her grandfather had once owned a carriage necessitates the upkeep of certain standards of respectability. Respectability is, after all, a thin path around the Abyss. The Respectable are able to hold their heads up high at the grocer's and the butcher's, and get credit, too. The Respectable do not find themselves turfed out on the street when they cannot pay the week's rent. The Respectable don't wake to the early morning knocks of the tallyman and the loanshark and the bookie's boy.

Dor, says Jane, when we start working, will we be rich?

Sure as eggs is eggs.

How rich?

So rich that we'll eat headcheese and corny beef and sweets.

They are walking along the towpath at Limehouse Cut, beside the gypsy boats with their brilliantly painted cabins.

When I'm rich I'm gonna walk through the door of Mrs Folkman's and say, So Mrs F, what have you got in today that is particularly good? And Mrs F will say, Well, Miss Fulcher, it's funny you ask because only this morning I made up a batch of violet crèmes and there's some splendid fudge an' all. And I'll say, Very good, Mrs F, top hole, make me up a half pound of both. I shall be paying, as usual, in cash.

Before the war Mark Moses turned out high class coats and bespoke suiting for the shops in the West End. His was one of the thousands of sweatshops littering the East End, but, unlike those which functioned solely as middlemen for the distribution of fabric cut-outs to women working from home, Moses employed a handful of men and women to work full-time in his premises and actually paid them a decent wage. It was a successful business, not that you would have known it from the premises, which were two filthy rooms above a grocer's shop in a terrace of black-bricked workshops and tiny factories. In the first of these rooms a dozen women sat in rows before treadled Singers and sewed piece-rate, the least experienced seaming linings and sewing gold galleon between the layers of coat fabric, and the most skilled working on buttons and hand-finishing cuffs and collars. In the second room pressers and basters hemmed and pressed the garments as they emerged from the machines, then hung them in steam to set the seams, and in a small antechamber between the two rooms a cutter laboured on the band-saw machine, cutting out pieces from stacks of cloth.

The worst of the sweaters treated their workers as little more than slaves, obliging them to pick up their cut-outs twice a day and paying them nothing for their trouble or their tram-fare. They demanded impossible deadlines and fined their workers for lateness, so that by the end of a week women who were working fifteen-hour days at their machines and travelling two or three hours to the sweatshops to pick up their pieces would find themselves only three or four shillings in pocket. From this they were expected to feed their families, buy their buttons and pay for their threads. The worst of the sweaters worked in cahoots with sewing machine salesmen. The salesmen would provide the sweaters' outworkers with machines on hire purchase, then, without warning, they would double the hire purchase rate and the sweater a cut. The buyer would eventually be unable to meet her payments, the salesman would then take it back, leaving the victim of his greed with no means of supporting herself or her children. Charles Dickens estimated that in his day between twenty-five and fifty per cent of the women working in sweatshops were resorting to prostitution in order to survive. Even so, there were many who favoured sewing over laundry work, which left you with leg ulcers and bronchitis, or packing flour in the mills where your lungs would bleed from the dust, or getting raw-skinned and stinking from the glue factory or half-crazed and fossy-jawed from the matchmaker's.

By the time my grandmother became a seamstress, sweating had improved a little. At least it was an established practice with established rules. None of the rules favoured the women who laboured at the machines, but there were rules, at least, and Moses, Quality Tailoring generally kept to them.

The following Friday afternoon, Jane and Dora return to the Mile End workshops.

A bulbous woman in a matt brown wig ushers them up the broken stairs with their covering of torn lino, and into the main workroom. Then she sets them down in front of a sewing machine and takes ten minutes explaining how to lift and drop the foot, how to feed in the fabric, thread the needle, control the speed of the sewing line with the treadle, and finally how to reinforce seams and remove the pins and basting. Then she hands each of the girls two small scraps of fabric and says she'll be back in ten minutes to inspect their work. For what seems like the longest while, the girls sit speechless before the pitiless contours of the machine.

Blow me if I know where to start, says Dora, poking cautiously at the needle. I ain't been this scared of nothing since me mum cut a loaf and there was a rat baked inside. But at least the rat was dead. She brings her foot hard down on the treadle and the needle begins a mad jerking. Janey, she says, we ain't never gonna be rich unless we get them seams done.

I think you 'ave to do it slower, Dor. With the greatest caution, Jane eases her foot on to the treadle, and the needle floats upwards. Like this.

Five minutes later Jane has put an elegant, forceful seam across the fabric.

How d'you get it straight, then? asks Dora, struggling with a fishing net of knotted threads. Finish this off before Mrs Wig comes back, will yer?

Right-o, Dor.

And Janey, you won't tell, will yer?

Jane Fulcher shakes her head and smiles.

Not in a million years, Dor.

The two girls clamber back down the broken stairs with the promise of a job picking pins and clearing away the threads for six shillings a week and all the sugared tea they can drink, start on Monday. At fourteen they can already see their adult lives stretching out before them: work, marriage, children, a home to look after, tea cosies to sew, and all Mrs Folkman's sweets they can manage. Marching across the Mile End Waste they feel as though they have grown a foot in an afternoon. They wander back down through the Waste Market, past stalls laden with ripe beef ribs and belly lamb, past trestles laid out with cabbages and haberdashery.

Stopping beside the beigel bakery, Dora whispers, Me dad says them Jew-boys is a bunch of cowards the way some of them have gone on the conscientious to get out of fighting. Me dad says they don't mind killing things when there's some killing to be done. To see them out on a weekday evening at the back of their little shops cutting creatures' throats and letting the blood run out and me' Dad says that ain't right. And most of them ain't half canny in the business way 'cos me dad says you can always strike a deal with a Jew-boy. She meanders on, but by now Jane isn't listening. She is thinking about six shillings a week and what you can buy for it if you get the bargaining right.

The afternoon turns out warm and bright. All along the route men are busy putting London back together, replacing bombed brickwork, boarding up shattered windows, tearing down the worst of the courts and alleys and clearing the empty plots for rebuild.

Let's check on the mooches and the gyppos, says Dora.

Me mum don't like us having nothing to do with them, Dor. Me mum says they're common as muck.

We can do what we like, says Dora, fingering her yellow hair.

Can we?

Course, we're in the money now, ain't we?

Strictly speaking they aren't in the money, at least not yet, and even when they are the whole lot will have to go towards the housekeeping. But these are minor details in the lives of two girls who have just discovered how to sew a seam and get paid for doing it. So they make their way down to the towpath that stretches across the Grand Union Canal to pass a few blank hours – some of the last blank hours of their childhood – spying on the gypsy men and women on their bright little houseboats, knowing as they do that the gypsy spells could turn them into cats or pigs at any moment, but reckoning that the gypsies' vilest spells and hexes are reserved for the ghosts of the men who drove them off the Plaistow marshes and sent them into exile here, on the canal, among the bodies of drowned dogs and the tide of human waste.

And after they've had their fill of gypsies, who look pretty much the same as anyone else when all is said and done, the two girls walk on across the cut to the Lea Bridge and join a grass path running parallel to the riverbank. To their left loom the lumbering Three Mills and to their right are the tanks and quays of the Bow Gasworks. This is not their customary terrain but this afternoon they are feeling saturated with the prospect of their future so they walk on regardless, heading east and leaving behind the grimy waters of the Lea. A gust of wind blows some putrid stink their way.

What's that smell? Not even the mooches smell that bad, says Jane.

They laugh and hold their breath until their faces go red as aniseed balls.

Must be the Outfall Sewer, says Dora. They sniff at the air, take in great gulps and swill it around their mouths like a fine champagne. And then they laugh and stamp on the grass path, the hot gusts of their giggles rising from their mouths.

'Ere, says Dora, we're laughing *like drains*.

The sound of their snorts and hoots catches in the westerly wind and whips east towards the sea.

Jane, says Dora, do you think we'll know one another always?

Well I ain't going nowhere, Dor. Are you?

CHAPTER 6

Into bloody everything the bloody Jews. Frenchie Fulcher lights a cigarette and exhales elegantly. Today he is in fighting mood.

They ain't into boat building much, says Sarah.

Ah no, says Frenchie, sucking on his cigarette, boat building is a skilled man's job.

They ain't into the docks much neither, Sarah reminds her husband.

Frenchie takes a pull on his fag and lifts his eyes to the ceiling. He can't win any argument over money with his wife, but that's no reason in Frenchie's mind not to have the argument.

Janey ain't working for a Jew, he says. Final.

Sarah Fulcher makes a show of clearing away the plates.

Hang on, says Frenchie, I ain't done. But Sarah keeps hold of her husband's plate.

A Jew's money's the same colour as anyone's. She has nothing against Jews. She feels sorry for them, whipped from their homes like common beggars and condemned to live in the courts and alleys of Aldgate and St George's when some of them, it was said, had owned carriages back in Russia. Besides she is a practical woman and a practical woman knows that with Frances Maud all set to marry, what they need is another income in the house, and another income is another income no matter from whose hands the money tumbles.

For her part, Jane knows better than to join in this argument so she sits at the fruit crate table with her sisters and little brother and hopes her father will disappear. She knows he won't, but she hopes it all the same because hope springs eternal and hers has sprung more eternal than most since making the vital discovery that the road to Selina Folkman's runs by way of Moses Quality Tailoring.

What are you makin' such a fuss about in the finish? says Sarah. The whole rag trade's a synagogue. Don't mean there ain't a wage to be had off it. And it ain't as if old Moses is coloured.

But Frenchie Fulcher just puffs on his cigarette, opens up his paper and shakes his head sadly, as if to say we're all doomed and it's words like that which doom us.

Twenty years of marriage to Frenchie has taught Sarah almost nothing about what makes her husband tick. But she understands enough to know that the quickest way to get him to stop ticking, moaning and everything else, is to set a plate of food before him. So she fills his plate with more potatoes from the pan and settles herself down with a mug of tea. And sure enough, Frenchie mumbles about Jew-Boys for a moment, then carefully pinches his cigarette behind his ear, sighs, picks up his spoon and lunges at his potatoes, and for a while something approaching peace settles on the room.

Of course Frenchie doesn't mean to ban his daughter from working for a Jew. What are Jews to him? Beigel-sellers, fruiterers, sweaters. Creatures to buy from and sell to. Not friends or relatives or loved ones, but men and women who, just like himself, have grown up in the shadow of hard and ill-rewarded labour. The working class works. That is the whole point. Work puts potatoes on the table and a roof over the house; work buys boots and beigels and keeps a fire burning in the grate; work pays for the doctor to come, and if it is too late, work provides the dead with a decent send-off; work is the thin seam keeping the working class from the workhouse. And Frenchie Fulcher senses that hard times are on their way again. The industries he knows – ship building, ironworking, ship repair – have been declining all around him. Of all the riverine industries, only the docks still flourish. And he wonders if the docks will be enough.

And so, on the Monday after her first sewing test, Jane begins at Mark Moses Tailors unopposed. Her first job is as clean-up girl, dusting down the bales of cloth as they come up from the store, wiping off any stray spiders and cobwebs and rat droppings, clearing threads that become tangled round the legs of tables and chairs, picking up pins, sweeping the floor of the furze left from the cutting and sewing of cloth, making tea and fetching, fetching, fetching: buttons, more cotton, another bale of cloth for the cutters, tailor's chalk and finishing threads. Her hours are from seven in the morning till seven at night, six days a week. For this Jane Fulcher takes home six shillings, rising to six shillings and sixpence after six months, less the price of any unaccounted for buttons, spools of thread and needles. Holidays are confined to Christmas Day, New Year's Day and May Day. Empire Day is not a holiday. Boxing Day is not a holiday.

By the end of the first week, Jane's skin is itchy with fabric dust and tailor's chalk, her eyes are balls of raw liver and she has tiny cuts all over her arms and legs. By the end of the tenth week her hands are already showing the first signs of rheumatism and they ache all day, the fingers as stiff as old sausages and the skin under her nails puffed with blood blisters where the pins have penetrated the soft insides. Her lungs are heavy with dust and she sometimes thinks it's a wonder she has any breath left for Sundays. The blaring heat from the gas-jet irons and the press of bodies (a dozen women and girls in a room fifteen-foot square) drains her youth away. Sometimes she feels so faint from the heat that her legs slip from under her and her frail body crumples to the floor. She has accidents this way, one time branding herself on the hot rack, a wormy burn the size of a fist swelling on her arm, another time tumbling on to a treadle and feeling the iron wheel thumping into her chest as heavy as a kick from a man in toecap boots. The thirst maddens her. By the end of the day all she can think about is a drink and how to get it. There is a standing tap at the corner of Layfield Place and most days, she and Dora run straight out after work and bury their faces in the water.

Look, I'm a river fish, says Jane, flapping her arms like fins with the armour of her hair lying wet against the sallow skin.

There ain't no fish in the river, says Dora, blowholing water.

What am I then? says Jane.

A bleedin' nuisance, says Dora.

If the bruises, burns and scrapes are bad enough, Jane's mother boils an onion and presses half on to the bruise or burn or scrape and the whole Fulcher family gets a bit of boiled onion for their tea.

All the same Jane is happy. For the first time in her life she has a little money, only a very little after Sarah has extracted most of it for housekeeping, but enough for a small bag of nut brittle, when she can get it, or a tiny phial of Devon violet scent. She likes to dab the scent behind her ears to ward off the smell of sweat and scorched dust, the reek of chemical dye and pressed cloth, the sour stench from leather trim and the metallic tang of needles. No, it's not so bad. At the beginning of the day when the sun is shining and she has a dab of Devon violet behind her ear and the taste of sweet tea in her mouth, and the women are chattering before settling down to work, it's not so bad at all. Tailoring holds a mirror to her life. The pattern is designed by an outside agency, the cloth is cut by a stranger, and she is left with the job of stitching it all together, putting in whatever tiny adjustments are necessary and possible and trying in the end to turn out something useful and pleasing from what are always secondhand beginnings. There are rules in the tailoring trade that aren't so unlike the ones she has to live by. There is a price to pay for profligacy or showiness of any kind. In tailoring, as in life, mistakes cost money, shortcuts cost money, doing anything differently costs money. What matters always is to be careful.

A few months pass and Mrs Wig offers Jane a position on the machines. You got the hands for it, says Mrs Wig, I can always tell when a girl has the hands. Could tell that from the very start. The war has ended now and Moses' is turning out civvie suits for middle class men. For a ha'penny a piece Jane hems collars, inserts the stiffening and closes them up. She works quickly and accurately. Her small, dextrous fingers are ideal for passing the cloth through the machine, particularly for detailed work where the fabric has to be manipulated round the needle. But the machines take their toll. The vibration gives her 'the tremble', so that she wobbles along the road as though she's a bit too fond of the bottle. Eventually, calluses the size of mothballs grow along her fingers which become immune to every pain except the constant thrum of rheumatism, but until then sores open constantly on her fingers. Her eyes, fixed on a line, cease to be able to move very easily from object to object. She finds it hard to focus and her head buzzes. The concentration required to keep the seams straight and the hands and feet working in regular rhythm frays her nerves. At night she slams awake with eyes blazing, convinced that some horror is about to overcome her. But in the greater scheme of the Abyss, these are only minor depredations. They aren't fatal, not yet. And you make sacrifices because you have to.

The simple pleasures of Sundays make up for the week. On

Sunday afternoons, Jane and Dora walk. Over the months and years of their early adult lives they walk the length and breadth and height and width of the great eastern haunches of the city. When the buildings are cloaked in fog and the rain is bashing at the bricks, they are still out on the streets, walking. In search of a cup of tea they will quite often drop in on Jane's relatives in Shoreditch and West Ham or on Dora's in Limehouse and Wapping. To reach the West Hammers, Jane and Dora must make their way along the East India Road to the bridge over the Lea at Bow Creek where, years before, Frenchie had pointed out his boats, the Maudie, the Edie and the Rosetta. The boats are no longer there now, of course, and nor is Frenchie. But they can still take in the thick, ripe odour of the air, a mix of tar from the boat yard and refining sugar. From this spot Tate and Lyle's refinery stands out like a great metal weed at the river's edge, and beside it Keiller's Marmalade and Trebor Sharpe's sweet manufacturer and all the other jam-makers and biscuit bakeries stretch along the wharves, turning the slub of marshy substrate at Silvertown into a sugar mile.

On 18 February 1920, Jane Fulcher turns seventeen. It is a particularly dreary morning and she is woken early by the cold. During the night her left foot has found its way out from under the bedclothes and the skin has grown swollen and beety, heralding chilblains. Trying not to wake Edie and Frances Maud sleeping beside her, she gets up, pulls on her coat and boots and goes out into the yard to the privy. Dust, the back yard dog, appears from nowhere and, slinking forward at a slope, displays his teeth and growls. Inside the privy the cistern spews shit-stained water over the bowl and on to the floor.

Happy Birthday to me, says Jane.

Back upstairs the family has risen. Sarah is mothering a thin flame in the grate, Frenchie is standing in his string vest smoking, Edie is dressing in Little Room and Artie is beside her, bouncing on the mattress.

Phew, what's that pong? says Frenchie. You brought the privy in.

Happy Birthday, Janey, says Sarah.

They sit down to their usual breakfast of bread and marg dunked in sweet tea.

Here go, says Sarah, handing Jane a package and a sixpence. Spend it on something nice for your hair.

Make the most of it anyway, says Frenchie, there'll be no more.

Jane arrives at Moses' earlier than usual, sits down at the treadle and begins her collars. All morning thoughts of the package and the sixpence in her pocket lead to wobbly seams and unfinished corners and overstiffened linings.

Just think of the sweets I can buy in Mrs Folkman's for sixpence, she says to herself, depositing another wretched-looking collar in the finishing basket. Pontefract cakes, honeycomb, Bassett's Liquorice Allsorts, Craven's Sugared Almonds, enough Sharps Toffee for a week.

By lunchtime the package is eating at her sanity, but to take it out in public would be suicide. Everyone would want a piece of what's inside. In the privacy of the back yard privy she unwraps the printed wax paper with its neat crease lines and air of newness, releasing the warm smell of chocolate and the aroma of rose Turkish Delight. Oh Miss Crème, she says to herself, you devil, and for fifteen minutes she sits there on the privy at Moses' sweatshop, transported beyond the East End to a place she had never been, where the air is soft and perfumed and life drifts by in a succession of signs and sun-kissed smiles.

The atmosphere at Ullin Street that night is tense, which is usually a sign that Frenchie and Sarah have had words over money. But tonight Frenchie is not there and Sarah is wearing a guilty expression, and if there is one thing Sarah is never guilty about it is money.

Janey pet, she says, drink your cuppa, then we'll be off.

Off where?

Off where you'll see.

It might be reasonable to imagine that Sarah would be taking her daughter on some surprise outing to celebrate the girl's birthday. But this is the East End in 1920 and there are no surprise outings, leastwise no celebratory ones, and even if there were, that would hardly explain Sarah's agitation as she puts on her coat and follows her daughter out of the door of number four Ullin Street.

The night is damp now, but their bellies are warm with tea and they appear to have a purpose, marching along St Leonard's Road, then turning west towards Chrisp Street where a few men stand quietly behind their market stalls and a few women still mill around in the hope of some day-end bargains. Sarah, who has said nothing all this way, now takes her daughter's hand and leads her through the alleys towards Limehouse, and finally to a dingy shop front whose glass has been partly covered with a large splinter of wood. They stop before the door and Jane glances enquiringly at her mother.

Shh, enough questions.

Inside is an oily wooden floor, a bell above the door, some broken shelving containing bottles, a few dilapidated rush chairs and a thin film of dirt embroidering everything. A metallic smell pervades the air.

Mum?

Shh, you'll see.

Hearing the bell, a stout man in his fifties emerges from the back room, his face scrubbed clean, the skin as red as cat's meat.

Ah, says the stout man, the young lady.

Well, says Sarah in an awkward tone, a mixture of guilt and overweening politeness. Well, I'll be off then.

The stout man continues to smile. Then he goes to a hook on the back of the front door and takes down a butcher's apron.

It takes three hours to pull out all the teeth in Jane Fulcher's mouth. Three-quarters of a century later she will still recall the head-popping splintering, like the sound of the earth cracking open. She will remember the blood and ruby spittle and the fragments of tooth falling from her lips, the mouth jammed with metal and the butcher's foot on her chest as he digs out her molars. The pain begins as a slow howl somewhere beneath or behind her stomach, which leaks into her extremities and finally wraps itself around her like seaweed, dragging her down into the pitch dark of nightmares.

The butcher's favoured tool for this operation is a monkey wrench, more commonly used for unscrewing rivets and rusty bolts. There is no anaesthetic. Jane is strapped into a chair with dockers' belts. Every so often an old woman appears and offers her a jar of cheap hooch and tells her to drink deep and stop making a fuss.

But it's hard not to make a fuss when blood is pouring down your neck and pooling in your lap. It's hard not to make a fuss when your lips are swelling and your cheeks are blowing up and your mouth has become an ugly tangle of red, housing gums so raw it feels as though they are about to burst and scatter the bits and pieces of your face across the floor. It goes on and on, the three longest hours of her life. She cries and sobs and shakes, begging for it to stop until the butcher threatens to give her a good clump over the head with his wrench to give her something to think about.

At the end of it all, stumbling from the greasy room on the arm of the butcher's wife, through well-worn and familiar streets, she cannot see through the monstrous throbbing in her head. She cannot speak or hear anything other than the sound of splintering. The butcher's wife tries and fails to comfort her.

She has the strangest feeling of absence. If someone were to stop and ask her name she wouldn't be able to summon it. Where's the comfort to be had when on your seventeenth birthday your mother delivers you to a butcher to pull out all your teeth? By the time the butcher's wife hands Jane over to her mother her face is a globe of raw liver.

Cup of tea, pet? her mother says. No? Well, then.

The Fulcher women sit in miserable silence for a moment then Frances Maud goes to fetch a measure of whisky from The Wellington. Sarah moves to wipe the tears galloping down her daughter's face and catching in the swollen corrals of her mouth.

I've sent Artie and John to yer cousin's in West Ham, she says. The girls will sleep with me tonight. Yer father will keep his hours in The Wellington for a day or two.

Edie begins to cry.

Oi, Edie, shut your trap. Janey's to have a drop of whisky and a good long sleep, says Sarah. She leans over and kisses the girl on the forehead.

I'll get Maudie to go round Dora's and ask her to come over tomorrow, cheer you up.

The whisky burns. Even then, half-dead with pain, Jane has no head for it. Her mother takes off her clothes and lays her on the mattress. She wants to say something (she doesn't know what) and tries to command her tongue but her lips are unruly squatters. With the index finger of her left hand she begins to draw the letters of a word, then remembers that her mother cannot read. Eventually she manages to whisper, Shug.

Sugar? You want sugar water? Her mother strokes the beads of sweat from her cheeks. You stay there, Janey pet, and I'll go and get you some.

Through the night Jane lies rigid on the mattress, drooling like a newly-knackered horse. Images play around in her head unsupervised. Sometime in the night her mother comes into the room and pours whisky down her throat and Jane sinks into a ragged sleep and dreams of spidery creatures and metal wrenches. The first thing she sees when she wakes is Dora sitting at the end of the bed, knitting. Somewhere outside a hymn is being sung. Is she awake or dreaming? She does a quick mental tour of her body which seems, for the most part, to be still there. She raises her hands to the emptiness of her mouth. The tune — she recognises it now — is 'Jerusalem' and the reason she can suddenly hear it inside the room is that Dora is singing along, only with different words.

Oh we lark down Poplar way
It's a cheery place to be
For they ain't too posh down Poplar Way
For the likes of you and me.

Ah Dora, Dora, she thinks, but her smile is turned away by her lips. She tries to speak, but what comes out sounds like the voice of a crust, like a crusty loaf speaking or a piece of coal.

Dora wheels round, winks. Our Janey, love, I thought you was never waking up.

Are, En?

Dora puts down her knitting, kisses her friend on the forehead.

I'll boil up some water, get you cleaned. You'll be right as rain in two flicks of a cat's tail.

Dora mops up the congealed blood with a rag, then the tiny splinters of tooth, picking at the crust of saliva with the nail of her little finger and still humming 'Jerusalem'. You must have known it was coming, Janey. I mean, what with Frances Maud having it done.

But no, Jane didn't know it was coming because no one had thought to tell her, and though she does recall, as a young girl, being sent away to spend a night or two with her cousins in West Ham and Frances Maud staying behind, she has never made the connection between this and the loss of Frances Maud's teeth. In her later years she always assumed her sister was born with teeth you took out. Until now, she has never been given any reason to doubt her version.

Maud's probably grateful now she's getting married an all, Dora says in an evasive tone, still wiping her friend.

Jane, allowing her head to nod a fraction, feels the rag pulling the clumps of blood stuck in her hair. Overnight her jaw has swollen and bruised and if she had a mirror nearby she would see that her face resembles an ill-formed turnip. What do Frances Maud's teeth have to do with marriage? And why is Dora such an expert on the subject? Some connection has passed her by. Again. In the way that connections do.

'Ere, says Dora, trying to be upbeat and salacious, you wanna know somefink my Annie told me? Remember that clean-up girl at work, wassername, the one what left a while ago, her cousin works on the machines? Well, my Annie says, that girl is in the bog one day, thinking she's got a bit of a blockage on. She's had a spoon or two of syrup of figs and she's sitting on the privy pushing like, and my Annie says she's pushing away and getting a bit sweaty under the collar when all of a sudden this thing come out and splashes right down into the toilet. Only the thing ain't the thing she thinks it is. This thing is a real live baby! Oh Gawd, now she's got a baby splashing around. So this girl gets up and she's screaming and carrying on, going God Almighty, Mary Mother of God, it ain't my baby, and they can't get no sense out of her at all and in the finish her dad has to break down the privy door and fish the poor little bugger out with his bare hand. And Annie says they was hoping it would die because it was born like a shit when you think about it, but it never done.

Dora picks up her knitting again.

Ooh, I wouldn't be in that girl's shoes. If she don't marry the father now, oh my lord there'll be trouble.

A resentful swell rises up in Jane's chest. What do babies in toilets have to do with it? She has no intention of having a baby in a toilet. For the remainder of the day she lies in bed while Dora reads her the scandal and murder stories from the weeklies, and wonders why it is there is so much rottenness in the world.

The next morning Jane shuffles to work with no teeth, her face as puffed as a cottage loaf and with Dora beside her, trying to shield her from the sight of her own reflection in the shop windows.

The pin-girl watches her taking off her coat.

Blimey, you had an accident?

The girls in the sewing room, older and wiser than the pin-girl, are kind enough to be short-sighted for the day. They've seen it before and they'll see it again.

Jane waits two weeks for the manholes in her mouth to seal and is then fitted with some porcelain teeth which make her feel she is chewing on tea cups. For weeks she cannot bear to approach a mirror, and when she does the face she sees is not her own. She thinks of a character for this new face, a dark, loathsome character, an awkward, ugly thing with its ill-fitting porcelain outfit. She comes up with Miss Chops. Poor Miss China Chops.

No explanation will really do. All the same, about a month after her birthday, the topic comes up in a conversation with Dora. They are talking about Frances Maud's wedding when Dora says, It ain't cheap getting married, is it? What with the bunch of flowers and what you got ter pay the vicar.

Oh, says Jane, don't you worry. Frances Maud's fancy man's got a bit of money.

That's the risk you take, says Dora, shrugging her shoulders.

What?

Well, says Dora, havin' yer teeth pulled then marrying a chap what's got the money anyway.

Jane wonders for a moment if Dora is playing some trick. But no, her friend's face is casual and her eyes direct.

Money for what? asks Jane.

What I mean is, it's a bit rich when you 'ave yer teeth pulled to save yer future hubbie the cost of the dentist and then you wind up with an old man who got the coinage to pay 'em anyway.

Jane isn't sure she understands. Does Dora think Sarah and Frenchie had their daughter's teeth removed to save her future husband money?

Her friend looks at her with a mixture of astonishment and guilt. Well why d'yer think?

A warm, breezy place in Jane's heart begins to cloud over then, leaving her with the lasting sense that if it were just her mouth which had been hollowed out it would be one thing, but other parts have gone too, parts that are less reachable and cannot be filled with dentures.

Sometime after that, my grandmother Jane did something very clever and very brave. Perhaps it was the bravest thing she did in her life.

Sensing that she had become a commodity whose worth appreciated in proportion to how much work she might do or how much money she might save, Jane Fulcher subverted the commodity and claimed it back for her own. She wanted no reminder of that day or the person it happened to. And so the person it happened to had to die and a new one had to take her place. She gave herself a new name. From then on, Jane became Jenny. Not so different, but different enough. From then on, there was no Plain Janeing Jenny because Jenny had a name of her own.

PART TWO

CHAPTER 7

It is a Saturday night and the young bloods from Barking, West Ham, Silvertown, Tidal Basin, Plaistow, Canning Town, Custom House, Beckton, Manor Park, Upton Park and Forest Gate are milling around the Premier Picturehouse in East Ham. Standing among the dandyish boys and dolled up girls is Jenny Fulcher, in a blue dress she made herself, with a brown gabardine coat topped off with a knitted cloche hat from which her thick hair peeps out. She is trying to put on a smile (though smiling often loosens her teeth and sometimes makes them pop out), but the brown leather shoes on her feet, her only pair, are pinching like a winter wind.

Suddenly there he is in front of her: Len Page. Her suitor. Her beau. Her knight in shining armour. Well, in a brown wool suit. How la-di-da he is, not handsome exactly, but strong and purposeful in his white shirt with collar and tie. His hair, a boiled brown colour, is groomed back with pomade. There is a starched and ironed handkerchief edging his pocket. His boots are polished so high you could start a fire with them. He is, it seems, the essence of respectability.

It's the Army in him, she thinks, this pride he takes.

'Lo, she says shyly, inspecting her shoes.

Well, you look a picture, he says.

Oh, she says. For a moment she thinks he has said 'you'll look at a picture' which is what they have come to do, then realising her mistake, she adds, I mean, do I?

Yes, he says.

Oh, she says, smoothing her hands down the sides of her coat and wondering whether he has noticed the little butterfly clip in her hair.

A dozen years have passed since Jenny Fulcher's teeth came out. John, Frances Maud and Edie have married and moved away. John and his wife live in Hackney, Frances Maud has gone to Barking and they never see Edie, the family beauty, whose husband swept her off to live in Nottingham where he is, of all things, a school-teacher. For the past five years Artie has been at sea. He comes home on leave from time to time but he can never wait to get back to his ship. You can't blame him. In the last decade it is fair to say that the senior Fulchers have been in decline. A chest complaint has left Sarah in fragile health and poor spirits. Frenchie has been unemployed. What little remained of the old ship-building industry in the East End has gone over to ship repair, and the ships are no longer wood but iron and steel. The ship yards don't need carpenters, and in particular they don't need ageing carpenters. Frenchie is reduced to sporadic work at the tea cooperage in the West India, making up barrels and crates, but the pay is poor and the old man misses the ships and the lighters and the dumb barges. Boat building was a man's job in a way that tea cooperage isn't. Men's lives are at stake when you build a boat. What is at stake in making tea crates?

Still living with her parents, it is left to Jenny to witness them crumble and, as often befalls the last girl left at home, to devote herself to their care. This is neither easy nor rewarding. The older her parents get the more exactly they require her time to be their time and sulk terribly if she is not there to serve them their tea and light their cigarettes and rub their feet on cold nights. Jenny's pleas for a free evening are met with dismay and an atmosphere of betrayal. In the great pool of their needs there are only reflections of themselves.

Will you leave us now, Janey, dear? asks Sarah.

It's Jenny now, Mum, and no, I won't leave yer.

And so she sits in, night after night, mending clothes and darning socks while Frenchie snores beside her in his chair and the hours trudge past like prisoners of war.

Home is no longer 4 Ullin Street, Poplar. Sometime between the teeth-pulling and the date at the East Ham Premier, the Fulchers moved to Caulfield Road, a leafier, less oppressive spot than Ullin Street in more prosperous East Ham. Unlike its neighbour, West Ham, which is heavily industrialised, East Ham is broadly residential, with a cramped, suburban feel. The district began life as a rural settlement of vegetable plots growing fresh greens for London's markets, but by my grandmother's day the city had grown over it, pushing the plots and allotments out to the fringes and depositing in their stead a tidy grid of terraced streets designed to house the respectable working class: foremen, dock gangers, tallymen, postmen, milkmen, clerks and bus drivers. East Ham's essential orderliness was nowhere more obvious than in the vast red-brick Town Hall with its attachment of slipper baths and the placement opposite – within view of the bathers as if to emphasise that cleanliness really is next to godliness – of an imposing stone church. But as the population of the East End swelled, so the houses in the perky terraces had been divided and the rooms sub-let and East Ham had taken on the feel of an ants' nest, as though the orderliness might at any time break open and be replaced by a kind of blind seething.

Caulfield Road, where the Fulchers lived, was a pleasant if

ordinary row of London two-up-two-downs. The houses were slightly bigger and better built than those in Poplar and now the Fulchers had use of the two downstairs rooms – a front room where Frenchie slept, and a living room with a fire where Jane and Sarah slept together on a roll-up mattress. There was a scullery as well as a yard. There was no bathroom, of course, no central heating, and only an outdoor toilet. Like most of the hutches built about the East End, the place was ridden with damp and bugs. All the same, it was a step up.

Sometime in her mid-twenties, Jenny realised it was possible to miss what you had never had. She had long given up on the promises Dora made when they were starting out at Moses' years before, but still she yearned for a home of her own, somewhere to be whatever it is she would be if she only had the opportunity, and a few things to put on the mantelpiece; some sweets and a sweet tin and a clock, maybe.

The only way you're going to get that is by finding yourself an old man, says Dora, who is long since married and has two children. And even then you gotta share it.

It isn't even that she hasn't tried to find a husband. Overcoming excruciating shyness and a chafing palate, she has managed quite successfully to smile at strangers and conduct stilted conversations with male cousins and neighbours and the brothers of friends, but with absolutely no success. The one or two oddballs who have asked her to the pictures turned out to be like raindrops that hang from park railings, accumulating water but never quite falling. She is afraid to count the times she has laid on her mattress in the living room with her mother's toes jammed in her face and her mother's snores rumbling like some fast-approaching thunder storm and prayed to God and anyone else who might be listening for a husband. Any husband. And now the years have rolled by and Jenny Fulcher finds herself still stuck at home with the bloom fading from her face and a pile of darning and not much prospect of another life. Until Len Page comes along.

Exactly how Len and Jenny met I don't know, but it wasn't so surprising that they did. Kempton Road, when Len was living, and Caulfield Road are just two streets apart. The pair would have walked along the same pavements, ridden the same buses, shopped in the same shops, bathed in those public baths overlooking the church.

At some point in the Twenties, Len had enlisted in the Army and had passed most of the flush of his youth in Burma, where he rose to the rank of Sergeant and gained a reputation for using his fists in the ring and out of it. While there he contracted malaria, and it was this, coupled with a number of mysterious disciplinary incidents, that had brought him back to East Ham. He returned to London with a plan and Jenny Fulcher fitted right into it. He, Leonard Page, was going up in the world. He was going up. And to go up, he needed a wife. A thrifty, obedient, loyal little wife.

I brung you these, says Len outside the Premier, handing Jenny a paper twist.

They raise their eyes to meet the other's. Jenny pokes open the bag and inspects the iced gems lying inside.

Want one?

Nah.

She pops a gem into her mouth and floats off into sugar heaven. They reach the head of the queue and the cashier says, Fourpence balcony seats or thru'penny stalls?

Two balcony, says Len.

Jenny stops sucking on her gem for a moment. Why waste tuppence? she says, removing two pennies from the pile on the counter. Yer backside don't know the difference. We could sit in the thru'pennies and make a tanner of it.

He smiles and squeezes her elbow with his hand. Jenny Fulcher, he says, you are a woman after me own heart.

Halfway through the film she has forgotten what they are watching. Something about a man who gets into a terrible mess with a train. Still, it's hard to concentrate. The actors have funny accents. She finds her eyes growing heavy. It's the new-fangledness of it all that bewilders her. Before the speakies came in, when you could read what the characters were saying, it didn't matter about the accents. She went to the pictures with Dora once, before Dora was married. It was better then. Those who couldn't read could always find someone to read the subtitles out to them and there was a kind of cheerful cacophony about the place. But really, it would be too rude to fall asleep. Len would think all manner of things and she wouldn't blame him. She reaches for the bag of iced gems and attempts to open it without making a noise.

Sssshh, hisses a woman beside them.

Len turns and frowns. A tiny vein of irritation beats on his temple. For a while Jenny withdraws her hand and tries to concentrate on the film with the opened bag of iced gems sitting prettily on her lap. But after half an hour she is driven by the irresistible force of sweetness to have another go. She pops one in her mouth, waiting for the moment the icing crumbles on to the tongue. Digging in the bag for another and holding it to the screen she whispers, as much to herself as anyone, Now, is this blackcurrant or strawberry?

Len's voice is raised just above a whisper now. If you don't like strawberry, spit it out.

I do like strawberry.

Oh shhh, why don't yer? This from the woman beside them.

Gawd and bleedn bennett, says Len. Will the bleedn saints pre-
serve us from the bleedn moans of bleedn women.

With the rain on their backs they splash out along the pavement
towards East Ham Town Hall.

Well then, Jenny, he says as they reach Caulfield Road. You got
any objections to the Dogs? 'Cos if you 'ave I won't take you, save
you moaning about it.

An image of Dust's teeth comes to mind.

Well, she says.

Dogs it is then, he says, definitively, backing off down the road.

She waits for him to leave, then rings the bell. Frenchie opens
the door.

You've been your time out here. What you been doing? He eyes
her from the side as he might a tart standing on a street corner.
Why didn't you bring him in for a cup of tea? Ashamed of us? Don't
I always say in by nine?

She hangs her coat on the peg beside the door and checks the
clock on the living room mantelpiece. Ten past nine. It is January
1932. In a month's time Jenny Fulcher will be twenty-nine years
old.

If you want to pinpoint the moment that it all began between
Len and Jenny, that instant when two lives ran into the same stream,
or perhaps the same gutter, the Dogs in January 1932 was probably
it. The track has gone now, demolished in 1972, but when Len and
Jenny met there it was the biggest attraction in the borough after
the Hammers football ground at Upton Park. On a weekend evening,
tens of thousands of men and women swung through the metal gates
to find their places beside the great ellipse of the track and tumble
with their luck.

He rings for her at six and they take the bus along the Barking
Road, Len smoking Seniors and rambling idly about dogs, saying,

A good little goer will hit thirty-seven mile an hour with no trouble, and jess keep going. So long as that hare's spinning round the track won't nothin' stop a good little goer. He'll be pounding that track till he falls down dead, the poor little sod. He don't know no different, see?

And Jane, sitting beside him, only half listening says, That don't sound very sensible.

A dog ain't sensible. A dog's a dog, innit?

Len flips another cigarette from his packet and lights it.

Hey, he says, cheery now, I seen people eat dogs in Burma. What do you say to that?

She tuts and shrugs a little.

Well, that's foreigners for you.

For Jenny the greyhound track is another world, a world she has read about in the *Mirror* but has never experienced, a world of glamour and high jinks and bright smiles, where women with fancy hairstyles chat to men in poplin suits, and couples eat shrimps with little wooden forks and their pinkie fingers stuck up in the air.

Where people have that elusive thing: Jenna Say Kwa.

Like it? Len asks, throwing his eye across the rows of benches, the standing area and down into the bookies' pit.

I don't know, she says, not so much because she doesn't but because no one except Dora and Rosie has ever asked her that question before.

They move up to the guard rail on the grandstand platform overlooking the track. For a moment she loses him in the jumbled flow of men making their way to the bookies' pit, then he appears again, bounding up the steps with a broad grin on his face.

What a bleedn shoe-in! The six dog placed in every race he's run this year. And he's at seven to bleedn one!

Oh, she says.

Port and lemonade? he says. Sweet sherry? Drop of gin?

I don't suppose they do a nice cup of tea, she says.

She watches him slice across the crowd, a lonely figure with boiled brown hair and the look of a man with something big on his mind. She can only imagine what his thoughts are.

In fact, though she doesn't know this, he is thinking about respect. To be precise, he is thinking about respect's constituent parts: rank and rules and fists. He is thinking about them because he fears that he may have lost sight of them. He has reached the bar now, and is waving an impatient hand at the barmaid with an eye on the men around him. Little men. He is thinking that to be sized up with these men seems a terrible injustice. To be compared. He, who earned his stripes in an infested swamp where people ate dogs; he, who paid for his stripes with malarial fevers, only to return home to discover that he is no more wanted, no more valued than the man who has never been further than this bar in this dog track in this grimy corner of the world.

So what can you do, Page? the man at the Labour Exchange had asked.

How can he say it? How can he say that he can survive dead-faced skies and throbbing heat, that he can march down dusty, pitted roads which peter out to half-macheted pathways through miles of stinking jungle. How can he say that he can spend months apart from any thing familiar, in the company of drifters and lost boys, and he can command these men and, above all, he can win their respect.

I can drive, sir, he had said.

Can you drive a trolleybus, Page?

I should think so, sir.

The barmaid catches his eye.

Fetch us a sweet sherry and a pint, love.

Right you are, soldier, she says. When it's your turn.

He stands apart from Jenny during the race, watching the lights dim, the hare begin its journey and the traps lift. She sees him leaning against the guard rail, sucking on his cigarette. The crowd howls. Heading down the back straight, the six is now two from the lead, taking the next bend at speed, elegantly hugging the rail. The lead dog suddenly fumbles, manages to right itself, but in so doing yields the lead to the three. The six, now second, moves towards the rail to take the next turn, leans in hard, looks like a dead cert, nudges into first place then bumps briefly with the three dog, stumbles, and in an instant the two dog thunders past them both and across the line.

In the finish, says Len, walking Jenny home along Caulfield Road, the trick is to pick the one what looks most hungry.

Hungry?

The dogs.

Oh, yes.

She remembers the first race and that tiny moment when the six dog lost the lead, that small moment of opportunity that it failed to grab.

Two weeks later, or perhaps it is a month, Len Page pays a visit to Frenchie Fulcher. They sit down in the front room on two fruit crate chairs while Jenny fetches a pot of tea. Both men know what this visit is about but only one of them welcomes it.

Len straightens his tie and smiles loosely.

Well, says Frenchie, spit it out. He draws himself back into his chair. The fire cracks and spits a red cinder on to the lino. Frenchie takes out his quarter ounce and offers it to Len and the two men retreat into the silence of the room. After what seems the longest time, Frenchie says, You've been a bloody long time coming. Listen,

Leonard, I don't mind saying, I'm not a young man and it's a hard life. He takes a drag on his cigarette and gazes into the coals. So what I'm saying, Leonard, is that family looks after its own, see? And I'm guessing that as from now, you're family.

On the morning of 25 September 1932, dressed in his good suit, Frenchie Fulcher walks the bride, Jenny Fulcher, from her home in Caulfield Road, along East Ham High Street to St Bartholomew's Church. The groom, Len Page, stands at the altar end of the church, dressed in a brown wool suit. The bride meets her groom in an ivory dress and with an expression of glazed astonishment. Frenchie follows a pace behind, a trembling, knotted hand clamped to his daughter as though trying to pull her back.

You might as well smile, girl, he says. But Jenny Fulcher does not smile because she is afraid that Miss China Chops might come bursting from her mouth and bounce prettily down the aisle to meet her groom.

The service is the usual Church of England homily, the vicar polite but from another universe, the sermon something appropriate to the occasion, the lilies of the field, perhaps, or the rich man and the eye of the needle. And then the thing is done.

Back at Caulfield Road, the wedding party drink beer brought in from an off-licence counter and eat sandwiches made with potted meat, and one by one the male guests press gifts of money into the groom's hands. The family presents and the bride's trousseau are brought out and thoroughly inspected. After that the guests start up a sing-song, but because there is no piano in Caulfield Road, they decamp to the pub where the men continue drinking beer and the women knock back port and gin and everyone gets merry and drinks toasts to the happy couple. After closing time, Len and Jenny make their way back to their new quarters in Altmore Avenue, about two streets away from the Page family home in Kempton Road and four from the Fulchers in Caulfield Road and a world away from both.

CHAPTER 8

On the morning of 26 September 1932, Jenny Page knocks on the door at Caulfield Road with a bag of clothes. Her mother, seeing her expression of damp misery and immediately guessing its cause, leads her into the front room, puts some water on to boil and sits her daughter down.

What's these tears, then, pet? Best you dry them. It ain't so bad, you know.

It is hard to believe my grandmother reached the age of twenty-nine knowing so little about sex. For much of her childhood she shared a room with her parents. When she was little she slept in their bed. Overcrowding made sex a public act. Even if she'd witnessed nothing at home, there were brothels down every lane and turning in Poplar. Whenever a large ship put into dock, prostitutes queued at the gates. Sailors would bet on the fights that broke out among them. Between times they hung around the seamen's missions and sailors' pubs. On the other hand few people spoke openly about sex and almost never named it. In conversations between women it was always 'the business' or 'the conjugals' or more common still, something unspecified that a man did to a woman, 'going near yer' or 'avin' his way'. You could be familiar with the code without having the least idea to what it referred. And that, at twenty-nine, was more or less where Jenny was.

Sarah Fulcher sits beside her daughter as she sobs her way through a cup of sweet tea then fetches her another. When that too has been drunk she squeezes her girl's gnarly hands and says, No questions, Miss Why, wives is wives and husbands is husbands and there's the end of it.

The end of it?

Yes, the end. Now, dry yer eyes and blow yer nose and go and cook your old man a nice spot of dinner.

And that is how the matter is settled.

Back at Altmore Avenue, there is a frigid atmosphere for a while and a touch of wounded pride. But it is gradually forgotten in the dips and swells of everyday routine and after a month or two, Len and Jenny settle down and for a while at least they are not unhappy.

Altmore Avenue was then, and still is, a long, straight, modest road of working class terraces lined by a stiff brigade of London plane trees. Until people discovered DIY in the Sixties and began building wonky porches and pebbledashing walls, every house was exactly the same. The regularity was welcoming in a place that harboured so much mess and chaos. The Pages take two downstairs rooms at number 27 for a rent of a pound a week. They are small rooms and ill-lit but there is a fire in each and a kitchener in the scullery. The floors are laid with lino, still quite serviceable, and the wallpaper is a pink sprig pattern which the damp has not yet turned yellow. As they sit in front of the fire of a chilling evening, it is gratifying to think that only weeks before they were a couple of oddballs, the bachelor Sergeant and the no-hope spinster, and now, with their new table and second-hand bed and bone-handled cutlery and hand-me-down china, they are just like everybody else – an East End Mr and Mrs Somebody in a sea of Mr and Mrs Similars.

Before long the neighbourhood wives begin looking in, bringing jugs of milk, little pieces of fancy soap or whatever offering will give them an excuse to knock on the door. Gossip slides in and out. According to Vi MacReady at number 25, Joey Hart at number 14 has a vicious temper and his wife, Annie, is one for the bottle. Annie says that Vi MacReady has had seven miscarriages and not all of 'em from Mickey MacReady neither, and that Mickey isn't averse to the odd adventure himself, but neither of them is anything compared to Susie Tipton at number 17. And Susie Tipton has nothing bad to say about anyone because nosiness is next to ungodliness and whatever anyone might say about her most of them ain't got nothing to crow about themselves, truth be known. Nothing to crow about at all.

A routine quickly emerges. Len is working shifts on the trolley buses from the station at Upton Park while Jane works at home, picking up piecework from Moses' and bringing it back to stitch. Two nights a week he spends the evening at the Upton Park bus garage, playing cards and chewing over dog form tables with his bus friends. On Tuesdays and Saturdays he goes down to the track to test the results of these discussions. Every other weekend, if he isn't working, he takes off into the country and shoots rabbits, whose ragged bodies she makes into hotpot and pie.

Jenny isn't unhappy with this arrangement. She is nearly thirty, after all, and has for a long time dismissed the idea of romance as something that happens in films. It is lonely, sitting at her hire purchase Singer and stitching collars and waiting for her husband to return home, often grumpy, to his tea, but there are worse lives, there certainly are.

At night she puts her teeth in a jar beside the bed. They undress in darkness. She spreads a hair net across her head and pulls on her bedsocks. Sometimes he touches her but never for long. Sometimes she says, Shall I put me teeth back in? but he does not seem bothered either way. He rarely kisses her.

She quickly learns that it is her job, the job of any wife, to blend her life into her husband's. This principle is no better demonstrated than in the business of the slice. Len likes his morning slice. And not just any old slice, but the right kind of slice fried in the right kind of way. Len's slice must be slice perfection, cut from half-stale bread, the middle section, before the crust tumbles down to meet the sides. The perfect slice has to be of the correct thickness, not so thick as a stack of four half crowns but thicker than three. It must be fried in lard which is not fresh but not yet rancid, preferably from bacon or gammon or even sausages, though chicken fat will do. Once the lard is hot but not yet quite bubbling, the slice can be placed flat down and then submerged. It must be fried for two minutes then turned and fried for a further two until it is the colour of a milky cup of tea. Only then can it be served, piping hot, with a little gravy if there is any, or salt if there is not.

In comparison to the daily preparation of the slice, every other domestic chore – the scrubbing and whitening of the doorstep, the blackening of the kitchener, the cleaning and oiling of the washing line, the banging of the rag rug, the feeding of the chickens in the back yard, the shopping and chopping and darning and cooking and mending – withers into insignificance.

What the bleedn hell is this? he'll say if the slice is at all altered from the norm.

A slice, Jenny will reply.

A *slice*, Len will say. Shoving the plate to the other side of the table, he'll continue, What colour do you call it?

Jenny will try to avoid his eyes. A bit on the dark side.

A bit bleedn dark?

Yes, she'll say, darkish.

Darkish my arse, he'll say. *This* . . . He'll hold up the slice by one corner, shaking his head as though revealing some national shame. This is bleedn black. You could put this on the bleedn fire and keep a family of bleedn eskimos warm for a bleedn week with this.

Well, she will say, struggling to calm the resentment rising in her voice, I ain't used to cooking slices. I gotta get used to it is all.

A bit bloody lucky you was never in the Army, he'll say with significance. Sorry, Captain, but I ain't used to ripping through the jungle, see, I wasn't brought up to bayonet Chinks what don't do as they're told. I gotta get used to it is all, he'll say, pushing away the plate. And then it will be time for him to go off to work and he will put on his coat and stomp down Altmore Avenue and she'll wait for him to leave before she lets the tears run out.

If it's not the slice, it will be something else. There is always someone or something to be angry about: the incompetence of greyhound trainers, the traffic on the trolleybus route, the slightly rancid smell of salt beef emanating from the beigel stall at the end of the road, the price of tickets at the pictures, Russian Jewish social clubs, vicars and other unspecified 'do gooders', anyone who tries to dodge their trolleybus fare, assorted traders and costermongers, and any man who has never been in the Army.

She tolerates it. She has to. That is how their marriage is: serviceable, decently made, the fabric compatible with the stitching, the whole reasonably if unadventurously cut out; not what you might call generous or elegant or stylish, but serviceable all the same.

Within five months Jenny is pregnant. Children have never been a part of her calculations. For as long as she can recall her only plan has been to leave Caulfield Road. Beyond that, her future has never interested her much. She looks forward to the baby in the way you look forward to anything pleasant and inevitable – Christmas, New Year, birthdays – with a smile on your face and a shrug. She takes it in her stride. It's just one of those things, like foggy days and frost in winter.

Jenny gives birth to a girl three weeks before Christmas, a bonny baby, dimpled and smelling of warm days, noisy like her father, as toothless as her mother and as stubborn as the both of them. The day later the neighbours are bringing round rock buns and bootees and little jackets fashioned from old aprons and shirts, and titbits of advice. She likes this. She needs the advice. If there are such creatures as natural mothers, Jenny is not one of them. The little body puzzles her. She wonders how to approach it. In the end she is drawn by the smell. She likes to hold the baby close to her face and suck in that smell, a luscious, soft aroma reminiscent of Turkish Delight.

She has no plans to expand her family but nature intervenes again and a couple of years later a baby boy follows and once more the neighbours are round bringing advice, bonnets and the rest of it, but this time the gifts are a little less generous and the advice more circumspect and gloomy. This has nothing to do with the boy, who is a smiling, amiable creature. It has to do with the Depression.

What a bewildering time it is. Women and children who only six months earlier were fat and ruddy, now slink around the market place hollow-eyed in the hope of picking up a mouldy apple or a rotten carrot or two. Men who have fought in the most terrible war the world has ever seen for the largest empire the world has ever known are reduced to queuing at the soup kitchens and relieving offices or hanging about in corners waiting for something to happen. Only the pubs do well. At closing, men in heavy boots roll out those who can no longer walk and leave them to pass the night dead drunk in the shadows. Politicians move in and make the most of the troubles, and in the absence of anything else to turn to, men and women turn to politics, collecting in the back rooms of the East End working clubs where in better times they did business with their bookies, and talking hard, political talk. For a while in the mid-Thirties, every public space seems taken up with communists, socialists and fascists sloganising in the parks, on the street corners. The political foment comes to a head in 1936, in Cable Street, Stepney, when the goosestepping acolytes of Oswald Mosley's British Union of Fascists and the Jews and radicals of the East End fight openly in the streets, driven from what might once have been a common goal by factionalism and poverty and the stark truth that there are no easy answers in the East End.

The effect of the Depression on the Pages is more subtle. They struggle but do not sink. Len makes a steady wage driving his trolleybuses. Jenny sews. They do not call attention to themselves. But the lying low runs against Len's nature and at night he breaks into rages, shouting for the babies to stop their noise. In all this uncertainty he feels trapped. Knowing how lucky he is scares him. The Fulchers are not so fortunate. The Depression hits them like a hot wind. Frenchie and John are out of work for years. Able and honest, they struggle to feed their families and themselves. The Depression makes desperate men of them. For Frenchie at least it is the end. An old man, aged beyond his years by hard work and disappointment, he can find no more stories to compensate him for a life that boils down to so very little. The fascists and communists are fighting in the street as Frenchie loses his battle. Perhaps he goes to his grave thinking about his family and the carriage they once owned. Perhaps he is just relieved.

From his seat on the trolleybus Len Page remembers Frenchie Fulcher's words: family looks after its own and from now on, you're family.

CHAPTER 9

A crystalline morning during the last spring of the 1930s finds Jenny Page heading up Altmore Avenue towards the High Street to fetch some bread. For months past all the talk in the Avenue and in the streets and suburbs beyond has been of war. But until this moment she has failed to take it in. The full sense of the war, its weightiness, has not permeated the everyday weft of her life. She has a habit of not thinking about anything unless she has to, with the exception of sweets, which she thinks about all the time. What brings it home to her, finally, is the cast-iron street sign at the top of Altmore Avenue. Or rather, the absence of the sign. In the High Street itself, the sign pointing the way to the library and the Town Hall, the bus stop plaques and the Victorian cast-iron hand that for as long as she can recall has pointed to the post office are gone, too. She prefers to live under the illusion that everything is the same. But this one tiny variation is enough to tell the whole terrible story. Soon, very soon now, they will be at war.

She crosses the familiar brown threshold of Smith's Bakers, and finding the place full of women with shopping baskets and determined faces, plants herself at the end of the queue. A few familiar heads nod and she nods back to them. She waits for a while, taking in the old scents of dough and toasted sugar, expecting a conversation to begin any minute on the subject of the signs, but none does. She wonders if she has made too much of it. For a moment she feels foolish. But the thought stays with her that once the signs are taken down, once the names go, then what is there to remind anyone they were ever there. Turning to an elderly man with a torn flat cap and the one-sided stoop of a docker, she says, I dunno as I can see how's a person s'posed to get around.

What? says the old man, clutching his ear.

What I'm saying is, how you supposed to get to Aldgate on the bus when there ain't no Aldgate? And when there ain't no Aldgate how d'yer know where the bus is goin'?

The old man just shrugs. Never go down that way so it don't bother me.

In the weeks that follow the daily newspapers are full of public announcements. Posters go up on every wall and window, leaflets slide through doors, and boys hold out flyers on the tube, offering tips on everything from gas masks to growing vegetables. This time round, at least, London has a sense of what it might be in for. Gossip spreads in waves, but what it boils down to is, how will it end?

Preparations begin. Each morning brings some small change, the gas lamps taken down or the windows of the shops boarded. All through the East End, volunteers dig up yards, lift concrete, carve allotments and tape up windows. Sandbags and tank traps close over the walls of municipal buildings and offices. The streets themselves resemble obstacle courses. Overground shelters go up as fast as weeds, home guarders dig defences and erect fences and sink pits in the soil. Trenches switchback across Lyle Park in Silvertown. The Royal Victoria Gardens' rose beds, which Jenny remembers from that last fine day before the Great War, are dug up and replaced with potatoes. Lone soldiers paint the red pillar boxes with custard yellow, gas-sensitive paint and the buses change colour too, from their habitual scarlet to the hue of London fog, like fruits un-ripening. Then they convert to gas and stop running late in the evening.

In Altmore Avenue women begin sewing blackout curtains while their men dig Anderson shelters. They no longer gather on the corners or sit on their steps peeling potatoes. Their children stop playing in the street. Old Eddie Tipton, patriot, devoted husband to Susie and sometime convicted moonshine brewer, spikes his front windowsill with tiny Union Jacks on knitting needles and blasts out patriotic songs by holding his phonograph out of the window. It does not escape the notice of the neighbours that the phonograph is never in evidence during Constable Fred Howe's daily perambulations in the area. Once PC Howe is gone, though, out it comes again, its tinny sound rousing and reassuring the residents of the Avenue who, in every other way, have nothing to feel reassured about. Everyone knows now that it is only a matter of time. Up and down the street families who have wireless sets sit huddled over the morning and evening broadcasts, waiting for the confirmation that the country is at war. A handful of men pack their bags and head off to the recruitment centres to volunteer, too restless to wait. Others sit tight for the postman and hope he won't be bringing call-up papers.

In the wealthier districts to the west of the city, whole populations decamp to the countryside or to friends and relatives in America, Canada, South Africa, New Zealand, India or Australia, shutting up their immense houses and dismissing their staff (or in some cases, taking them along). For East Enders there is little prospect of escape. Only a few have relatives or friends elsewhere. They are stuck with it.

Week after week drags on without a declaration, while somewhere distant German tanks rumble across wooded valleys flush with summer, and Chamberlain shuffles to and fro making promises he cannot keep. And then, finally, the war is declared on 3 September 1939, and for weeks after families sit tensed in their homes waiting for the first conflagrations. Months pass with no significant threat to the capital. If they are at war, *where is it?* The word you hear on the streets and in the shops and pubs is phoney. A phoney war.

The blackout fuels the feeling of disorientation. On moonlit nights the streets are a forest of stone monoliths, gilded in silver plate. In the deep void of the blackout, everyone feels lost. Thin phalanxes of timid walkers tiptoe gingerly behind whoever among them is in possession of a torch, too terrified to strike out on their own. Some walk round in circles, others head off in the wrong direction only to discover their mistake when they are miles from home. Treacherous and invisible in the night, the river takes to swallowing its own. Every week Londoners topple over the keeper walls into the grimy water, only to be dragged out, lifeless, in the dawn. And when it is not drowning Londoners, the river is drawing a map of their whereabouts. In moonlight it glows like a silver arrow, lighting the way for German bombers. Londoners begin to turn against their own river, forgetting that for the past thousand years it has cleansed and transported and watered them.

For some, life blooms in the darkness. Away from the glare of the street lamps, scores are settled, alliances are made and deals are done. Money changes hands, pockets are picked, sex is bought and sold, goods are smuggled and every evening brings some new adventure.

One night in October, just after the war has begun, Len swings open the door to Altmore Avenue, his breath heavy with beer and in his arms a set of overalls and a lumpy kit bag.

Under the Spreading Chestnut Tree
Neville Chamberlain said to me
If you want to get yer gas masks free
Join the bleeding ARP

He slings the overalls across the table and gives his wife the look of a man who has found his place in life.

So I did, he says. He sits down at his usual chair, takes a long sip of tea and proceeds to tuck into the faggot and potatoes she has put on the table.

Blimey, she says. Well I never.

I've been thinking, he says, through mouthfuls. A man's gotta be ready to take what's his. He begins spooning the gravy on his plate with his customary speed. Know what? A line of gravy escapes from the side of his mouth unnoticed. A chap come up to me in the street the other day and says, Look here, my son, we ain't never more than four meals from revolution. The way I see it with this war is, he swallows a forkful of potato and begins on a slice of faggot, it's an opportunity. And with that he shoves his empty plate across the table, plucks a Senior Service stub from its rest behind his ear, sucks the smoke deep into his lungs and smiles like a Crown Prince about to inherit a kingdom.

For Len Page the war is a shot in the arm. His heart stirs with ambition. He is thirty-six years old and in a reserved occupation. His fighting days are over. Like some nocturnal thing, stretching itself awake at dusk, he prepares for the hours of darkness. For the first time since that day on The Upminster speeding into London, he is engaged and hungry-eyed. Somewhere in his deeper reaches he senses this is his chance. It is about to be Len Page's war.

For weeks Jenny barely sees him, but when he is at home he's all cheerful distraction and busy industry. The angry Len Page is gone and a new, cheerful Len makes life in Altmore Avenue oddly pleasant. He jokes and tells stories, invents nicknames for his fellow busmen and for his colleagues in the ARP, even takes some interest in his children. Hey nippers, he says to them one night, guess what? On account of the war, my bus ain't gonna run on petrol no more.

Unused to their father's attentions, the children stop the ball game they are playing and shoot nervous glances at one another, wondering if this is a test.

What's it gonna run on then? asks the girl.

Nice, juicy little 'uns.

The children glance at one another.

No it's not, says the girl finally, backing towards the door.

Oh yes it is!

No it's not! giggles the boy.

And with that Len reaches to grab them but they skate away and tumble laughing into the corridor.

The Air Raid Precautions was the best thing that happened to my grandfather. It got him about and helped him make connections. Patrolling the streets, knocking on doors, chaperoning anxious children and lonely women, he wove every detail of his new life into the pattern of his ambition. The ARP gave him what he was looking for. It gave him respect. Up to that moment he had been a chancer whose chance had not yet come. In the course of his ARP duties he was able to branch out, spread his wings and establish himself, indisputably and for the first time in his life, as king of his manor. Opportunity didn't have to knock on Len Page's door. He let it straight in.

Rationing, curfew, blackout. These were the early miseries of the phoney war and Len circumvented all of them. Whatever anyone on his patch needed or desired — petrol, stockings, a bit of warm-hearted company — Len knew where to get it for them. He was fast becoming a bewildering enlargement of the man Jenny thought she knew. She would only have to walk down the street and some stranger would come up to her and press a note into her hand and ask her to pass it on to Len. It was as though in the midst of a drought someone had poured fertiliser on him and given him a good watering.

Sometime soon after his ascent to the ARP, Len brings back a glued, hardcover notebook and from then on, whenever he is at home during the long years of the war, he enters figures into that notebook, adding and subtracting and establishing inventories and tallies and lists of who knows what. It doesn't take a genius to guess that the ARP isn't the only business Len Page is in. Jenny is in no doubt that her husband is making money. It's not that she sees any of it, but she can feel it in his smile, in the way he throws open his paper, eats his meals. Food begins piling up in the cupboard under the stairs – corned beef, sardines, packets of dried peas, then lamps, candles, pieces of tarpaulin, empty bottles, men's knitted gloves, soap, leather goods. He acquires a lock for the cupboard then, when it is full, he begins filling the Anderson shelter, and acquires a lock for that too.

The first Christmas of the war he takes them to the busmen's party over in the garage at Upton Park. In past years, Len has been reluctant to take his family at all, as though he considered them to be no credit to him. This year it is different. Sitting on the bus on their way to Upton Park he is bouncing the boy on his lap and his eyes are shining.

The Upton Park bus station building is a spacious, Edwardian red-brick structure. From here, buses fan out across the East End. In honour of Christmas the busmen have decorated their machines with handkerchiefs and paper tassles cut from newspaper. Women in dresses and men in shirt sleeves mill about, sipping the watery beer and swapping union tales and notes about the prices of things. In a corner at the far end of the building, the men have set up a makeshift playground for their children, with balls and a rope swing.

Jenny Page takes a seat and watches her children skip across to the playground. A woman beside her starts a conversation about rationing and for a while she drifts in and out, wondering if there is anything sweet to be had. At some point during the evening a young woman with honey blonde hair passes around tiny fondant fancies and it is just as she is about to raise one to her mouth that Jenny notices Len at the far end of the building pushing their daughter on the rope swing. The girl is smiling, her mouth wide open to catch the whipping breeze, and he is smiling too, pushing her a little higher each time. She is laughing now, and bouncing in the seat. And he is pushing her so high now that the swing looks as though it might shear from its keep and the girl is no longer smiling or laughing, she is trying to turn her head to face her father and it is clear that she is afraid. Len carries on swinging with a faraway look on his face. Jenny stands, unevenly, and begins to move towards the swing, slowly, then faster, but before she reaches them a timid-looking man has taken hold of the ropes and is gradually bringing the swing to a halt. Then the honey blonde woman is beside Jenny saying, You didn't eat your fancy so I brought it. She hears her voice, far-off, make some meaningless response but her thoughts are all on Len Page and in her mind's eye is a remembrance of the small smile that played about his face as he pushed the swing.

CHAPTER 10

Before the declaration of war, a letter arrives. In the Page household a letter is something of an event. This one, printed on thin, off-white paper, the blanks carelessly inked in, breaks unexpected news. The War Office is evacuating Jenny Page and the boy to Billericay, South Essex. They are to be billeted to a farming couple, the Berrys. Mr Berry will meet them off the train. The girl can remain in London, pending further instructions. Jenny turns the note over in her hands, reads it once more. She can barely make it out, the way people speak now, all *pending*, *notwithstanding*, *heretofore*. But the message is unequivocal. Well then, she thinks, with a floating sense of dread. The country.

The news sends Len into a powerful rage. Who'll do the washing? Who'll look after the girl and see to his tea? He'll not do a woman's job. Has the whole world gone topsy turvy? It's the men who are supposed to be sent away in wartime. The *men*. The women's job is to stay put and wait for them. That is simply the way the world is. After a few hours in the pub he reconsiders the world. His mother, Emily, says she'll visit Altmore Avenue twice a week to give the place a scrub down and see to the washing. The girl will go to a cousin's for a while. He will take his meals in the busman's café at Upton Park and the rest will have to wait.

Jenny worries that she will miss the kitchener and the warm smell of home. She worries that she will miss the city and her daughter. She worries whether she will miss her husband.

Seven years of wedded blisters! she says to Dora one afternoon in the run up to her departure. It don't seem like it was yesterday that we was eating iced gems down the pictures. She takes a sip of tea then it strikes her that there never was a *we* eating iced gems down the pictures; it was only ever *her*.

And so the time comes to leave, and a clear, cold day late in the autumn in 1939 finds Jenny and the boy at Liverpool Street Station.

Number five for Billericay, says an ancient uniformed porter.

How long does it take to get there, mister?

The man shrugs and waves his hands in the air in a vague gesture of defeat.

This is the same Billericay as what's in the country, ain't it? says Jenny.

The very same, missus, the porter nods, sure of his ground.

Mothers sit amongst their cases, rocking gripey toddlers or clasping babies to their chests. For the most part they are younger than Jenny and facing war for the first time. The air is filled with the sound of reckless chatter about billets and rations and whether you can buy soap or tea or a drop of jam in the country. Before them at the buffers stands the train, a green engine pulling maroon carriages. Here and there people are already boarding. Jenny finds a spot next to the window in a half-empty carriage and settles them both in, folding their shabby coats and placing them on the rack above the seat. She considers what she knows about the country from Len and realises how little that is. She imagines a great wodge of land called 'the country', filled with mud and scurrying things. Beyond that it's a blank. Do they have shops? Or muffin men? Or postboxes? Can you buy soap there? And tea? And jam? She imagines, for a moment, a life without jam. Her stomach aches at the thought.

A plump woman takes the seat beside her, settles her baby to her chest and nods towards the boy. He's a dear thing. Bless him.

He has his moments.

Evacuating?

S'pose.

Ah. The woman nods sympathetically. Where you going?

Billericay. (Even the word sounds foreign.)

Then the whistle is blown and there is a last-minute clattering of doors before the train begins to ease itself from the station. They trundle past the stone piles of Shoreditch Town Hall, across the lanes and turnings of Bethnal Green, past the burial grounds and the London Hospital then over the Grand Union Canal. They grind to a halt for an instant beside the Georgian terraces of Bow, where Frenchie's family once kept a carriage, then creep on towards the Lea and out into the Essex marshes.

She thinks of Frenchie. Poor Frenchie. The world left him behind. The world will leave her behind too, but she won't mind as much as Frenchie did.

They speed through outer London, the respectable working class suburbs of Ilford, Barking, Romford and Hornchurch rising before them and racing away. An unfamiliar green appears outside the window, then a confusion of branches glowing in the late afternoon light like iron railings. The train slips into Billericay just as the sun is disappearing. Jenny wakes the boy, nods a farewell to her travel companion and clambers down the iron step on to the platform where a dozen men and women are standing waiting for their charges. Anyone for Page? No one speaks up. Settling the boy on a bench outside the ticket office, she meanders along the platform in the final trembling of the light. Then the sun slides and it grows colder and dark. Nothing for it but to wait, she thinks. Waiting is what she is good at. Stars begin to brighten in the sky, such a profusion of stars, enough to fill Trafalgar Square a hundred thousand times. She wonders if the country is always this silent, this un-regarding.

Half an hour later, Mr Berry finally appears and, giving no expla-nation for his lateness, bundles her, the boy and their sacking bag on to the front bench of an old-fashioned trap. He whips up his pony and they clatter along a metalled road, and after a series of turns find themselves on a chalk surface which glimmers in the moonlight like a mouldy bone.

The trap pitches and wakes the boy, who begins to cry. It is cold, so much colder than the city and the air smells of nothing.

Mrs Berry and me, we dunno much about children, don't have none ourselves, says the old man. His tone is resentful. Can you milk?

She shakes her head.

Plant?

She smiles awkwardly and catches his eye. He turns to her and, not unkindly, says, Well, we'll just have to make a countrywoman of yer somehow.

The wind picks up and clears the clouds from the moon. Berry sets the trap along a tiny lane surrounded by thick hedges and they carry on in silence for a while, falling further into the depths of the trees. Before long, a small red-brick house appears and they emerge in a little hollow with the fields opening around them like the pages of a newspaper.

You'd best come in then, says Berry, leaving Jenny to carry her bag. Inside, the cottage is low and cramped. A wood fire is burning out in the grate and the air smells of damp and must. Snuffling, the boy reaches for his mother's coat.

Shh now, snaps Berry. Mrs Berry is gone to bed already. I'll see you to your room.

They climb a short, narrow staircase leading to a tiny pyramid under the eaves. Beside the door is a straw mattress and next to that an oak washing stand with a jug of cold water sitting inside it. Curtains made from pig feed sacks hang at the window.

Hope you brung soap, Berry says, only we ain't running a charity. And with that he is gone.

Jenny puts the boy to bed, washes at the oak stand and lies on the straw mattress in her liberty bodice, listening to the sound of Berry's footsteps and the creak of a door below. The house falls into a penetrating silence. A feeling of fatigue overwhelms her, but just as she is about to meander into sleep, a wretched howl starts up somewhere outside. She waits for the sound to melt back into the darkness. A profound silence falls once more. Something begins scraping on the roof. All night, the noises of animals pick at her sleep. At some point before dawn she is dazzled into a thin doze and wakes what seems like only moments later to the sound of a cockerel crowing across the emptiness. The tiny room is powdery with dawn. She draws the curtain and lets in a thump of frosty air. Beyond the hedges and the flinted expanses of the fields she sees the day drawing itself up from the east like a genie in the mist.

Mr Berry turns out to be an amiable, if mostly absent host, but from the start of their stay his wife resents her guests and openly complains about the burden of their upkeep, though she is swift enough to find Jenny employment about the house and farm. The routine at the Berry farmhouse is unvarying and implacable. Every day, including Sundays, Mr Berry rises and leaves the house shortly after dawn. Mrs Berry follows him out to draw water from the well then busies herself with the goats and pigs, returning to the house just before eight to get breakfast — a bowl of oat porridge and a mug of sweet tea plus a boiled egg for Mr Berry. After breakfast she settles to the household chores. Berry arrives back at the house around twelve-twenty and ten minutes after that Mrs Berry serves lunch – usually some kind of watery stew with a slice or two of bread. Meals are an odd affair, with Berry never putting fork to mouth until his wife has picked over his plate and described its contents. Mr Berry, she'll say (Mrs Berry calls her husband Mr Berry. He calls her Mrs Berry and, in unguarded moments, mother), Mr Berry, them 'taters is lovely and floury today and that cabbage is as fresh as can be and that's a nice piece of pig belly in there, lots of salty fat on that one. Once this routine is done, the pair gobble their meal in silence. Then Berry rises from the table, puts on his flat cap and boots and is gone. The lunch is cleared away and the afternoon begins.

Mrs Page, says Mrs Berry, knocking on the attic door at five-thirty on the first morning, what with the help gone off we'll not be short of things for you to do. We start the day early here in the country.

Jenny's first chore is to fetch water from the outside well. When she has hauled three or four buckets and put them in the copper to heat, there is the hay to fork, the cow teats to clean off and milk, the shed shit to be shovelled, the eggs to be collected, the hens to feed, the coops to scoop, more water to be hauled from the well, the household laundry to scrub, the whites to blue and the collars to starch and the cottons to put through the mangle, and in-between times the boy to dress and feed and watch over.

They eat supper together at six. The meal consists of bread and jam with perhaps a piece of cheese for the women and a slice of corned beef or a piece of faggot for Berry. There will usually be some dour conversation on the subject of whey washing or scrapie. Mr Berry will place one last log on the fire and Mrs Berry will settle to some needlework or book-keeping and a kind of inertia will fall on the house. At seven Mr Berry will do a tour of the farm to bolt everything down for the night. By eight-thirty the Berrys will be in bed, in separate rooms, and after nine the house will again be as still as pond water. Once in a while in the night Mr Berry will make odd heaving noises and Jenny will hear Mrs Berry calling to him.

All right Mr B, nothing to worry about. Everything's all right.

The dripping branches and silent, deadly afternoons begin to chip at Jenny's heart. She is used to the familiar East End stench of chemicals and coal smuts; the earthy smells of the country seem unnatural to her. At night the awful echoing and scraping sounds keep her awake and by day the lonely, voiceless lanes and fat, stinking cows freeze her blood. The solid, homogeneous food (gruel, bread and drip, cabbages, weak, undifferentiated stew and nothing even remotely sweet) and the unimaginable cold (and it is only November) make her long for spewing chimneys and a bowl of liver and onion. And there is the house itself, creaking and consumptive. A house that appears to float on mud. When she opens the curtains in the morning, there it is, a sapping, relentless mud sea. After six weeks she has had enough.

Mr and Mrs Berry, she says one day at supper, I reckon we'll be going back home.

They are eating bread and marg, and Mr Berry has a plate of mutton stew in front of him which Mrs Berry is in the process of describing.

What, says Mrs Berry, when we've only just got used to yer?

Jenny shrugs.

Sweet tender little bit of carrot in there, Mr Berry, says Mrs Berry.

It's ess that we ain't used to the noises, the mud an' that, says Jenny. We're used to London, see?

Lovely piece of fat on that mutton, Mr Berry. All pearly. Smells like the hay just cut. Mrs Berry goes over to the tea pot and pours a single cup. The Berrys will be obliged to put up someone else, of course.

Oh, well, Mrs Page, she says in a curt voice, if that's how you feel there's no arguing with you. Go back to Lonnon then and get yer two selves bombed to bits.

At the end of the week Mr Berry gives Jenny and the boy a lift to the station in his trap. They pass by the now-familiar flinty fields and spiky trees but at the top of the lane they are overtaken by an unfamiliar smell.

What's the stink, Mr B? asks Jenny. It ain't half powerful.

Mr Berry shrugs, points to his nose and makes some reply that is blown away by the wind. Turning a corner, they run up hard against a tractor pulling a trailer of manure.

Blimey, Mr Berry, says Jenny, holding her nose, you must be able ter smell it now! I never stunk nothin' so bad.

The pony turns to the right and slows to a walk.

Can't smell nor taste a thing, says Berry, finally, tapping his nose again. Gassed in the war you see.

They plod along the approach road to the station and Berry holds the pony while Jenny carries the boy and the sacking bag from the front bench and deposits them on a strip of paving beside the station gate.

Good luck, says Berry, whipping up the pony. They watch the little trap recede into the distance. It is a twenty-five minute wait for the London train.

Back in London, there are queues everywhere and the shops appear almost empty. The East End has become a place of women. There are fewer buses, and blackout blinds or curtains hang at every window. Altmore Avenue is lumpier, the gardens having been dug up for Anderson shelters. Inside number 27 the rooms are coated in coal dust, the bed is unmade and there is a pile of dirty washing on the kitchen floor. There are tins of dried milk and corned beef and packets of pearl barley everywhere. In places the tins are stacked into towers, and the towers of tins lined up one against the other to form tin cities, divided by highways of dried peas.

Len seems pleased to see them, though he's too busy to take much account. What's going on here is a man's business and none of yours, he warns. So don't ask.

London is thinning out. Within a week of Jenny's return, Artie Fulcher is drafted. A few days later Tom Page volunteers. Another printed letter arrives requesting that the Page children report to the Evacuation Board. Jenny Page makes her way across the rugged landscape of words. *Heretofore, thereafter, pending further instructions.* She recalls the men in uniform marching along the East India Dock Road, the red, white and blue bunting flapping idly in the slipstream of artillery carriages and the sense that it would all be over in a few months. She packs her children's few belongings in the sacking bag and reminds them to wash their necks and do a nit check on Sundays. Then she watches them board their train at Liverpool Street Station, the little girl clasping her brother's hand, and wonders when they will be home. Every week she expects them. The months pass in a state of waiting.

On 24 August 1940, the sirens begin to sing as they do from time to time, and as usual Jenny Page makes her way down into the Anderson shelter. She pretends not to be afraid, which is harder on your own than in company, and a few minutes later she hears the soft fall of incendiaries followed by a rush like the passing of some giant arrow. She takes a humbug from the jar on the shelf – only one per air raid – and sucks hard. The following day she walks down to the Town Hall and volunteers to firewatch. She cannot know that the London of her childhood is about to be blown into the history books.

CHAPTER 11

Mr and Mrs MacReady scurry out into the yard, blinking from their Saturday afternoon nap, and stand there, motionless, with their mouths dropped like horses' gobs.

Well ain't that a thing, says Mickey MacReady finally, and me thinking it was the wireless.

Several doors down, at number 27, Jenny Page and the upstairs lodger are also in their yard, looking up at the sky to the east, where one hundred and fifty Heinkel and Dornier bombers covered by a drift of Messerschmidts mass towards London.

What we supposed to do now? says the lodger.

A shadow sails above the roof tops. It is the most unthinkably beautiful thing they have ever seen. For reasons she neither understands nor has time to unravel, Jenny is suddenly struck by an overwhelming urge to talk to Frenchie, to be with him. It hits at her heart so directly she feels weak with it. Trying to move, she goes nowhere. She hears the lodger saying something and feels his hand on her arm but her body is planted in the ground. The porcelain plate inside her mouth chafes against her tongue and brings her sharply to her senses. How could she have been so muddled? Frenchie? It's too late for Frenchie. Frenchie is dead. It's her mother she wants.

On Altmore Avenue men and women are scattering like human

filings. Jenny can feel herself trembling. They are all trembling. Even the street is shaking.

The buzzing noise is getting louder now, nearly drowning out the whistles and shouts and protestations of the people in the street. Jenny quickens her pace, the breath punching her chest, and starts running along the High Street towards Caulfield Road, passing frightened women and old men tumbling in the opposite direction towards the tube station. From somewhere along a sidestreet an ARP man is shouting, To your shelters! The stragglers begin to panic, racing along and leaving their abandoned shopping bags to tip their contents into the road. Cabbages roll along, seeming to join the flow.

Just as her legs start to buckle, she reaches 147 Caulfield Road and, bursting through the door, sees Sarah, frail and taut-faced, standing beside the bed with a blanket in one hand. The old woman stares at her daughter, disbelieving.

Oh God, Janey, Janey, what'll we come to?

I'm here, Mum, says Jenny. Grabbing the blanket, she bundles her mother into the cupboard under the stairs and there they crouch, hunched and with their heads bowed for a long moment, panting and trying to retrieve their breath. The sound of engines bears down on them. Remembering the paraffin lamp that Frenchie always kept on the shelf, Jenny strikes a match. The flame sends a guttering glow around the black outlines of their bodies. There is nothing to be done but to wait for whatever it is. Bombs? Incendiaries? Gas? Sarah is moaning now, her eyes closed, hands rocking and her face leaking tears while her daughter squeezes beside her, feeling the bones of her buttocks and the aching, arthritic nubs of her knuckles. From somewhere quite close there comes an unmistakable thud and a slight tremor, as though the foot of some giant creature had just imprinted itself in the yard outside.

Oh my lord, cries Sarah.

The thudding sound repeats itself only more loudly. A smell of sweat moves around the cupboard. The old woman's shoulders are shaking uncontrollably now and she starts to cry again.

Mum, Mum, don't cry, whispers her daughter. I can't do nothing for us, Mum. What can I do?

Sarah's sobs only grow louder. Jenny lifts her hands to her mother's face, but the old woman pushes them away, so she transfers them to her pockets to stop the shaking. Inside the fabric, something small and hard and sticky touches the fingers of her right hand. Barley sugar she thinks, ah, *barley sugar*. Its presence comforts her. For an instant her lips curl into a smile.

Then another bomb thuds down somewhere close, followed by a shower of breaking glass.

Oh God, oh my God, we'll be buried alive, cries Sarah. Janey love, Janey?

Yes Mum, whispers Jenny, shocked by the fright in her voice.

I ain't half scared, Janey.

The daughter reaches out and grasps her mother's hand. I know, she says. She pulls out the barley sugar from her pocket and dusts it down with her fingers. Have a sweet, Mum. She posts the barley sugar into her mother's mouth and watches the old woman suckle on it, the dear old face trembling. They sit like that for a moment, in the small, peaceful deep of the understairs cupboard while the thumps carry on, but fainter now, coming from somewhere further south.

The docks, sighs Sarah.

For a long while they sit, grateful for the silent nothingness and faint damp tang of the cupboard.

'Ere, whispers Sarah finally, you had any of them bangers from Paterson's?

Jenny glances at the sagging figure of her mother, trying to gauge the woman's mood.

Why now, Mum?

They was letting 'em out generous with the coupons. I thought there must be something wrong with 'em, says Sarah, ignoring her daughter's question. Yer father would have said, don't trust 'em, pet, we'll go without. We ain't eating no iffy bangers, he would have said. Not for no money. You know that? It wouldn't surprise me if they was made of nag's meat.

You reckon?

Have you seen 'em? Awful dark they are.

From somewhere very distant there comes the crack of anti-aircraft fire.

Sarah takes another hard suck on her barley sugar and shakes her head. Awful dark.

At six-thirty pm the all-clear sounds. They wait a while for luck then emerge into the dimming day. Others are already out on the street, wandering aimlessly, as though they no longer recognise their surroundings. There are groans and sighs and the sound, somewhere, of shrill laughter. At number 145, a group of men and women have already gathered around a wireless and are waiting for the next news bulletin.

Oh Sarah and Jenny Fulcher, says a voice, ain't this a terrible business. Come in. A man with a clipped BBC accent announces a newsflash and begins listing bomb damage in West Ham and round the docks, saying there are casualties. Someone in the crowd snorts at that and says quietly, Oh really? However hard Jenny listens, she cannot take in what is being said. There is a fuzzy pressure in her ears and her legs have cramped from the crouching. In the middle of the newsflash someone passes her a jar of tea and it is only then, seeing the tea jiggle in the jar, that she realises how hard she is shaking.

All around them in the street, their initial shock collapsing, women are crying and swapping stories with an air of relief mixed with dread for the next time. Well, I better get back home, says Jenny. They walk slowly back to number 147. At the door, Sarah takes out a handkerchief and begins dabbing her eyes.

Don't leave me till your sister gets here, Janey. Only it has been an awful shock.

Later, halfway down Altmore Avenue, sensing someone behind her, Jenny turns and finds Len bowling down the pavement in his ARP overalls.

Well they done it now, he says, eyes shining. Half Silvertown and Canning Town come down. The Hammers was playing at Upton Park. Versus Spurs. Terrible mess with the crowd. I gotta have me tea and get back there.

Jenny puts on a pan to heat some water while Len checks his boxes of this and that in the cupboard under the stairs and comes back saying there's a packet of tea missing.

I ain't had it.

Well it ain't there. He sits, contemplating the situation. Oh, that's right. He wags a finger in the air. That Paterson had it, the butcher.

He raises his mug of tea and is about to put it to his lips when the sirens start up again. She watches the tea trickle back down his chin. A look of sympathetic weariness passes between them.

How much of this we gonna get? he says, throwing on his coat.

A minute later he is back with a grin on his face.

Ain't got time to get back down West Ham way, but come and see this, old girl. Come and see old Tipton.

There he is out in the street, shaking his phonograph towards the sky and shouting like a madman into the trumpet.

It ain't here you want, not here. You want the Aldgate. The Yids are down the Aldgate way.

For the following eight hours the Pages and the upstairs lodger lie huddled in the Anderson shelter while the sky above them roars and burns and whistles. After an hour or so the men take to playing gin rummy but it's a poor game. The bombs go on and on, each crack, every thud some new devastation.

It'll be the docks again, says Len. Down Silvertown way. If I know the British Army . . . he tails off.

There in the Andy, surrounded by the raging of the bombs, no one knows anything about the British Army. No one knows anything about anything any more.

The all-clear sounds, finally, at four-thirty am. They come up to the surface squinting like moles and smelling of mud.

Breakfast then, says Len, and I'll be off.

After he has gone Jenny sits down to write a letter to the children, moved by the sense that what is happening requires a record of some kind. But what do you say? Dear nippers, yer mum and dad got that bit closer to being blown apart today. After trying a few versions, she gives up. At seven or thereabouts, Dora knocks on the door and lets herself in.

Blimey. Poplar ain't so bleedn popular today. Ain't hardly nothing left of it. You and yours all right? She gives her friend a pinch on the cheek.

As right as.

Me mum's nerves are in bits.

I'll put on a cuppa.

Dora takes off her coat, sits down and lights a cigarette.

I thought if you wasn't doing anything we might take a gander at the damage. We could take a walk down Silvertown way.

Oh I dunno, says Jenny, I got collars to sew.

Ah, go on. The Nasties ain't gonna come back today, the bastards.

They take off towards the river. At Canning Town, by the Rathbone Street Market, they stumble on a great spray of broken

glass, and in-between the shards, blown leaves and the bodies of
birds and rats and the odd cat or raddled-looking dog. They carry
on in the middle of the road where the glass is most thinly scattered,
turning west and south along Tolgate Road towards Custom House
and the Royal Docks. Here the road gives out to dust piled in sallow
grey mounds, dampened by overnight drizzle, tucked into every
windless nook and corner and heaped like cake flour at the edges
of buildings. The air is heavy with it, despite the rain. At Regent
Lane the buildings are frayed about the edges. Crimble's Housewares
is now open to the world, its housewares slung across the road and
an incident team already clambering through the mess. A middle-
aged man in uniform approaches them and asks for their identity
cards, rubbing his eyes from the cordite. Behind him, two fire
auxiliaries and an incident officer are taking notes.

What's the damage, mister? asks Dora.

Not too bad up here. But Silvertown — what a mess.

They turn into Stansfield Road, but find themselves blocked by
a makeshift barrier, behind which another incident team are turning
through the skeletons of the row of houses, stripped of their frontage
to expose blackened kitchens and a front room complete with aspidis-
tra but with the wallpaper hanging in strips from the wall. Jenny
and Dora gawp through the dust towards the blue light of the
incident officer. On the other side of the road two houses lean on
one another in complete collapse. The air smells strongly of gas.
Dora begins to cough and lights a cigarette to ease it.

What happened here?

The incident officer, an elderly man with a walrus moustache,
shakes his head. Enemy strafed the area with incendiaries and used
the firelight to target heavy explosives. Most of this is fire damage.
Look at them houses, opened up like cans.

Don't suppose the contents are still alive? asks Dora.

The incident officer points to a six-foot-high dome of what looks like clay and turns out on closer inspection to be compacted debris — clothes, brick, roofing tiles, a lampshade.

Under that pile, we think.

They have never seen anything like this, have never even imagined it. Brick and mortar simply blown away and men and women blown away with it. A griping kind of sickness rises in them and a deep dread of what is to come.

Need help getting that pile sorted? Dora asks.

Wouldn't say no.

The compacting makes the job slow and hard work. Others join in until there are six volunteers digging from the sides of the mound inwards, lifting planks of wood, clothes and a washing copper from the mud and brick. The smell of gas and the choking dust are almost unbearable. Still they lift and haul and shovel, powered by the sense that in another day or another week, somewhere around the city a group might be gathered around a mound digging out *their* friend, *their* mother, *their* child. That is what they have learned during the night. Jenny wonders what everyone is supposed to do. Go round each other's houses every day to check who is still alive? And with her mother already halfway round the bend from worry.

After an hour or so of digging, a tiny lump of a hand appears out of the mud. They dig around it, but when they get to the wrist, it separates from the mud and comes away. It's a man's hand with the wristwatch still attached.

Oh God, says one of the incident team, a fellow in his fifties with the bent legs of rickets and the beginnings of something in his throat, perhaps a goitre.

They are tired now, feeling spent, each taking it in turns to break off. They stretch their arms and down a proffered cup of hot, sweet tea. There is grim work to be done. Strength sapped, spirits worse, they set to the heap again and pull the handless man's body from the rubble. Under it they find the body of a woman, and under her a baby, both dead and stiffening. Someone begins the job of cleaning up the bodies with a broom and a bucket of water while the rickety fellow thanks everyone for their help and makes a few entries in his log book.

A couple of nights later, one hundred and seventy-one bombers flew over London. Four hundred were left dead. The day after that two hundred bombers pummelled the streets in broad daylight and another one hundred and seventy dropped bombs through the night, leaving three hundred and seventy dead. On 10 September St Katharine's Dock was razed, melted wax from the warehouses leaking into the quays, sealing the river with a hard crust. Hundreds more died that night. And so it went on, and on, and on, night after night, the East End seized by the pounding of bombs and screeching of incendiaries and puk-puking of anti-aircraft fire. The fragments of shells clattered on to roofs like metal rain, debris piling up in residential streets to window height. Rubble was strewn along every major street, and between the remains of buildings lay tank bafflers that had been blown along like tumbleweed. Shops and homes gaped like mouths, fires sprang up. Smoke from bombs, smoke from fires, smoke from factories, smoke from anti-aircraft guns and planes and flares and vehicles stuck to the surfaces of buildings, the clothes, the skin, the lungs. Drains burst, gas pipes leaked, the whole unseen subterranean world of tunnels and wires seemed under constant threat of collapse. On the surface, sandbags, wood shards, glass, brick, even tree branches obscured roads and passageways. At the Thames itself, parts of the embankment crumbled away, ancient wooden quays collapsed or burned black, jetties fell into the riverbed, the river water pushing ash and oil and tarry waste and plaster and brick and pieces of wood and the odd body east towards the sea. Day after day the East End bore witness to its own destruction. Everywhere there was dust and the inescapable tang of cordite. Churchill said that Londoners could take it. But it wasn't Londoners who were taking it. It was the East End.

All through the Blitz, the rich lived on in a world more or less unblemished by the bombs. Sometimes it seemed to East Enders that the war had reached as far as the Tower of London, then given up and gone home. They imagined a world Up West where men and women dressed for dinner and went to fancy restaurants and ate steak and creamy puddings then passed round bottles of port and danced to the sounds of polite orchestras which drowned out the other, more distant, sound of bombs falling not three miles away, where other men and women were growing gaunt from malnutrition, overwork and despair.

In fact, the city's infrastructure had collapsed almost overnight, and not only in the East End. In a matter of days from the start of the Blitz the civil administration of London almost disappeared. Sewers went unrepaired, electricity cables spat sparks into the streets, and it became impossible to get any works authorised let alone completed. People were left unpaid, certificates unsigned, births and deaths unregistered. Within a few weeks, forty per cent of the houses in Stepney, built by unscrupulous speculators on marshy ground, had simply fallen down. The streets weren't far from anarchy. There was covert but widespread looting and anything untended disappeared. Desperate women picked through the rubble looking for coins or tins, knowing they could be fined or sent to jail for looting but driven to take the risk all the same. Hundreds crowded into the tube and set up camp there, saying it was no longer safe to remain above ground. They had a point. Above-ground shelters proved hopelessly inadequate. Some collapsed without any bomb ever having fallen near them. The sense of impending doom was magnified by food and water shortages. In the East End, life became very stark, a coarse scramble for food and money.

Despite the best efforts of the clear-up teams, there was rubble everywhere and, in among the rubble, rats and putrefying body parts. From time to time, after a bombing raid, the trees would be covered in ribbons of human flesh and the streets would run pink with blood. Down by the river, the high tide brought in sea debris and the low tide left bodies on the foreshore. In parts of the East End the vibrations from bombing raids were so bad that coffins rose up to the surface of the cemeteries and spilled their contents. You didn't want to find yourself beside a church for fear of what you might see.

The air was humid, thick with dust, and quickly became home to dense swarms of mosquitoes which flew alongside the buses, worrying the passengers. A West Ham jam factory was blown up, spilling sweet stickiness across a half-mile radius, and within a day, such clouds of flies rose from it you could barely walk through the area without choking on them. After that the Northern Outfall Sewer was breached, sending a flood of raw sewage into the River Lea, contaminating several food processing factories, a meat packer's and a chemical plant. For two weeks the smell was excruciating. Anyone living or working within a mile of the breach could taste the shit in their mouths. Typhoid, diphtheria and gastro-enteritis crept back into the city. There was talk of a cholera epidemic. Conditions were worse than they had been even in the darkest corner of the nineteenth century.

About two months into the bombardment, Jenny is in the back yard digging winter cabbages when Mrs MacReady's head appears above the yard fence.

'Ere, Mrs P, says Mrs MacReady, it's Mr Mac, he's having a turn.

Jenny shakes the earth from her fingers. What type of turn?

I'll come round, says Mrs MacReady.

A minute later she is at the door.

Oh Mrs P, he's been like it all week, I dunno what to do with the bugger.

Jenny digs the dirt from under her nails and puts on a cup of tea. Yesterday's leaves, powdered milk. There is no sugar.

I don't suppose you'll have a biscuit, says Mrs MacReady.

I don't suppose I will.

Only I thought – Mrs McReady leans in confidentially – with your hubbie's connections.

The thing about Mr P's connections, Mrs Mac, is that they don't connect in my way.

Mrs MacReady nods thoughtfully and appears to accept this as some intimate, women's secret.

I don't suppose you'd have a bite of bread and drip then, Mrs P? The old are always at the end of the queue, in spite of which it was us what won the last war.

Speaking of the old, says Jenny, ignoring the question, what about Mr Mac, ain't it about time we went round?

Oh, he ain't going nowhere. Mrs MacReady waves her hands. Now if you could get us that drop of bread and drip, Mrs P?

In spite of the chaos of the previous few months, nothing could have prepared Jenny for the sight of the MacReadys'. Every spare receptacle, including pots and pans, has been put to use as a chamber pot, filled and left around. There are old tea leaves scattered about and what looks like cat shit on the floor. The dust of months covers every surface. Where's Mr Mac then? asks Jenny, unable to see a space big enough to store a man.

In the cupboard.

There she finds him, unwashed, smelly and huddled up like a beetle, wearing his outdoor clothes and a gas mask.

Mr MacReady, says Jenny, I don't know why you don't come down to number 27 and have a cup of tea *and a drop of bread and scrape*. She shouts this last, remembering that Mr MacReady is hard of hearing. Back when all this started — it seems an age ago — he thought the sound of German bombers was interference on his wireless.

No, I ain't leaving, grunts Mr MacReady.

He won't listen or nothing, tuts Mrs MacReady. He ain't eaten nor drunk, ain't slep for weeks neither. The old woman bites her lip.

Jenny studies the man in the cupboard for a moment. His eyes are rubies, hard and red. The skin on his face is yellow with wear. He has the mean look of the sleepless. It's a look you see all over the East End. From time to time even the strongest of them has it. You can get used to the taste of powdered egg, pea flour soup, whale meat rissoles, you can manage the stomach cramps and diarrhoea, the acidity, ulcers, pasty skin and weight loss. It is even, after a while, possible to cope with the daily threat and presence of death. But the lack of sleep drives you almost insane. The dreadful lying awake, night after night, listening to the thundering bombs and the pup-pup-pupping of anti-aircraft fire and the buildings falling like horses at the knacker's yard.

Jenny reaches out a hand and gently pulls on Mr MacReady's elbow but the old man stays where he is.

Come out and have a cuppa, Mr MacReady.

I ain't going to die for them Jew-boys, snarls Mr MacReady.

Now, Mr Mac, what kind of thing is that to say? asks his wife, reaching out a hand for the old man to brush away.

Sometime the following day a nurse takes Mr MacReady away in an ambulance, and that's the last time Jenny Page ever sees her neighbour. Another casualty of the war, but one who will never make the honours lists or be remembered at the Tomb of the Unknown Soldier or be buried with flags in some neatly mown cemetery.

From her firewatching post Jenny Page witnesses the transformation of the city. Four nights a week she surveys her patch from the roof of an old factory building – sector 13, post 4, an arc extending from Custom House to the borders of West Ham and Silvertown. For the first time in her life she finds herself above the city looking down on it, instead of being always in its shadow. What a size London is! Even from the top of a building it is impossible to see its edges. On nights when the tide is low and the moon is full the bombers come whining and throbbing along the path of the river, the searchlights raised to pick them out. She listens to the anti-aircraft guns, follows the paths of the tracers. Over the months she watches her city burn. A gin factory goes up, producing flames as blue as the summer sky, another night bombers target the timberyards at Surrey Quays, the heat from the flames blistering the fireboats on the river. She watches warehouses at West India Dock flare up like roman candles.

One night in the spring of 1941 the bombers appear and, buzzing up the Thames, release their arsenal over Silvertown. It is one of Jenny's firewatching nights and at the sound of the air raid siren she rushes down the long flights of steps to the factory cellar which serves as a makeshift shelter. When all-clear rings she scrambles up the stairs on to the roof to check for fires. The instant she opens the door to the roof she is hit by the strongest, oddest smell. To the south, at Silvertown, a sheet of transparent blue flame shivers across the Thames, sending waves of warmth and a tart, throat-clenching odour towards them. There is a quality to the smell she recognises. She thinks for a moment, trying to place it. Of course! Sugar. The blue flame floating above the Thames is burning sugar. The sugar mile is a mile of flames.

CHAPTER 12

By spring 1941, Emily Page has lost three children.

In early June 1940, three months before the start of the Blitz, a telegram arrived at Kempton Road. *Regret to inform . . . your son Thomas James Page . . . on active service . . . during the evacuation of Dunkirk.* He was forty years old.

Six months later, during one of the daytime bombardments of the East End by German bombers, a high explosive bomb scores a direct hit on the shoe shop in East Ham High Street, scattering glass and shoes on to neighbouring roofs and the branches of nearby trees and killing everyone in the shop outright, including shop assistants Daisy and Ria Page.

The only surviving casualty of these two events is Emily. Her husband, Jim Page, has long since lost his mind. The move to the city proved too much for him. Sometime after the first war Jim collapsed and was dispatched to an insane asylum where he now passes the days alternately strapped to a bed and wandering about the wards begging his fellow patients to help him with the harvesting, unable to recall his name or the sound of the wind in his beloved Essex fields.

Packing away her clothes and linen between mothballs in the cupboard, Emily Page meets the world in black. Insensible with grief, the old woman forgets to eat. Within weeks she has halved in size and her face has shrunk to a skull. For a while, the neighbours, worried for her health, take to dropping in with little gifts – a jug of soup, a handful of currants. She greets them as a living memento mori. After many strangled attempts at conversation, they leave, awkward and embarrassed. In a few months, they stop coming altogether. For a while she moves into Altmore Avenue. Though she has never made a secret of her disdain for her daughter-in-law, she needs her now. Each night she sleeps in the bed with Jenny while Len camps out in the chair in the kitchen. Her confused night-time perambulations drive Jenny and Len to distraction. One time they find her in the Andy, another time in the downstairs cupboard, on a third occasion a neighbour calls to say she is wander-ing down the street. Her days consist of bitter rantings – the bed is too soft, she misses her own room, Jenny's cooking turns her stomach, the house (though identical to her own) is colder and draughtier. In short, she wants to go home.

Back in the gloom of Kempton Road, she begins to imagine her children will return. Each morning she wanders down to what remains of the shoe shop and sits on the pavement outside, waiting for the answer that will bring her girls tripping around the corner. Knocking on her neighbour's door she asks to listen to the wireless for news bulletins of her boy. And then, after many months and many bulletins, it finally occurs to her that she is going about this the wrong way. To get her boy and girls back all she has to do is find the person responsible for their disappearance. In the dark hours she runs through the list of possible candidates. If only Daisy and Ria's husbands had not allowed their wives to go out to work! If only Len had stood up and fought instead of cowering in the safety of a reserved occupation! If only Jim had not snatched them from their rural idyll (in her grief she forgets cruel winters, the endless mud, the impossibility of earning a living and, above all, how much she hated it) and brought them to this monstrous city, which even as she sits mourning her babies, is falling down around her. Weighing up the culpable, she decides that Jim is the real Judas. Was it not enough to bring them here to die? He had to turn his back on reality and on them, too.

In this atmosphere, it isn't so surprising that Len Page chooses to keep his feelings about the deaths of his brother and two sisters to himself. Watching him eating his breakfast in the mornings, Jenny tries to imagine his suffering, or at least to imagine that he is suffering, but if there are turbulent seas in Len's heart, he has built a pretty good sea wall to keep them in.

Two incidents give him away. Emily has gone back to Kempton Road and he and Jenny are once again alone. It is a Saturday and he has just come off his bus shift and is sitting in front of his tea in the kitchen in Altmore Avenue. They are eating pea flour soup but he has barely tasted his when, without any warning, he puts down his spoon and, grabbing the bowl by the rim, shoves it violently across the table towards Jenny. Then, without another word, he rises from the table, takes his coat and cap down from the hook and charges from the room. Moments later she hears the door slam.

Later that night, returning from her firewatching duties, she opens the front door, turns to close it and becomes conscious of an odd noise coming from the kitchen. Since Emily's stay, Len has taken to sleeping on the chair in the kitchen and she assumes at first that the noises are the sound of his snores. It is only as she reaches the kitchen door and stands quietly outside that she realises the snores are the sound of Len's sobs. She can hear him softly calling Tommy, oh Christ, Tommy. For an instant she puts her hand on the door knob, thinking to go in and comfort him, but all of a sudden the sobs cease. Withdrawing her hand, she retreats to the front room, takes off her clothes, removes her teeth and falls into a thin sleep, woken every so often by the sound of Len calling for his brother, over and over, through the still hours of the night. At dawn she gets up and makes her way in the darkness to the kitchen, only to find he has already gone. Heading back into the house from the privy, she notices the door to the chicken coop is open and there are feathers lying around the doorway. Inside is a scene of devastation. Chickens are scattered all over the coop, their necks broken and their stiffening bodies left where they fell from their executioner's hands. She gathers a few in her arms and holds them to her chest and remembers the cat in Ullin Street and Frenchie waiting to be put out of his misery.

A month or two after the twins' deaths she is sitting at Frenchie's table, sewing, when a sudden feeling of emptiness sends her to the Coleman's mustard tin on the second shelf above the kitchener. She see-saws off the lid and peers in. Inside are two barley sugars and a couple of ancient aniseed twists, her emergency rations. She puts the lid back on and pats the tin. She sits back down to her sewing machine and begins putting the top stitching on a collar when the threads begin to take on a shape. An outline emerges of a head, then hair, nose, a pair of smiling eyes, and suddenly there is the face of someone she recognises and does not want to see. She muzzes up the thread and works on, pulling the fabric of the collar across the treadle foot, but the face reasserts itself and before long it is there again, only this time bigger and more detailed.

Go away, Rosie, she says, feeling a wetness scrambling down her cheeks. Go back home.

She goes into the front room and sits on the bed for a moment. Not wanting to venture back into the kitchen just yet, she looks around for a distraction, lights on a pencil and decides to finish a letter to her boy and girl.

Dear You Two,

I hope you are both keeping very warm and being polite and
grateful and you are not getting into no trouble and that you, M,
are holding your brother's hand on the way to school which is a
long way I know but we all have to do our best in times like
these. And don't be giving them old ladies no lip because old
ladies must be respected no matter what, and always take your
syrup of figs but don't be greedy and swallow too much or you
will suffer terrible gut ache and I hope you remember London
and your home. There is no news here except your Aunt Daisy
and your Aunt Ria have gone away but I am here still and so is
your father.

Be good.

With love from your mum

She studies the looping words and sees the gaps glaring back
at her. Just before bedtime she steals out to the Andy to fetch a
sugar cube from one of Leonard's boxes, thinking she will just take
one. She roots through dried milk, canned corned beef and packets
of pea, wheat and potato flour but finds nothing sweet. Resigning
herself to an unsweetened night-time cuppa, she pushes on the
Andy door but the padlock outside has caught on the corrugated
iron and the whole thing is stuck. Looking around for some kind
of lever, she finds a piece of metal bracing among the boxes and,
holding the torch under her arm, attempts to crank open the door
with the metal strip but to no avail. She slumps back on to the
makeshift bench and tries to calm herself. Most likely the sirens will
go off tonight and the lodger will come down to the Andy and by
dawn she will be back in her own bed. She sits and waits. But the
sirens do not go off that night. Many hours later she hears the back
door open and the sound of the lodger's footsteps in the yard.

Suddenly, there is his face peering at her from the brightness of the day.

I come down to use the privy and saw the back door was open, he says. You all right?

He pulls her up into the yard.

A brick come off something and got stuck under the door, he says, glancing awkwardly at the hand still clinging to his own. You poor thing. Can I get you a cuppa?

She shakes her head. He puts an arm around her and squeezes her shoulders. There, there, no need to cry, pet.

But it is too late. There is so much to cry for. For the war and her absent children, and for Rosie and for Daisy and Ria and Tom and Mrs Folkman's confectionery shop, and for Frenchie and the little eyeless cat in Ullin Street.

The following day, she returns from her firewatch before dawn, lights the grate and draws the blackouts. A freezing fog licks around the house, rendering it looming and abstract. Len comes in at first light with brick dust in his hair and ears, his face the colour of the mudbank.

I'll see if there's an egg, she says, turning away from the keen edge of his mood. Scraping a pyramid of chicken shit from the wooden toilet seat in the privy, which is doubling as a makeshift chicken coop until the weather shifts, she finds an egg behind the S bend and reminds herself to get some carbolic from the Town Hall, since they are giving it out free.

She lifts a single rasher of fatty bacon from its newspaper wrapper, lays it in the pan and cracks over the egg, the smell of the meat sending her back before the war. She cuts a slice of bread and lays it in the pan to catch the grease. Nice bit of bacon, she says, but he doesn't reply. It is not unusual for him to ignore her, but there is a special quality of ignoring today, a more profound silence. He looks soft-faced and shabby in his ARP gear. She wonders who he has pulled from the rubble, who he has rescued and who he has failed to save. He eats conspicuously, flooding his chin with bacon fat while she drinks her first cup of tea of the morning and tries not to catch his eye. Poor Len, no kin left in the world except the old woman. Ah, she thinks, Len, no man deserves that, not even a bleedn cuss like you. Washing the last of the egg down with sweet tea he says, American.

What?

The bacon.

She pours him another cup of tea but he's disappeared into the place in his head where things get thrown around.

Yank bacon, Yankish marg, Yank coming out me bleedn ears.

She clears her side of the table, lifts the machine on to it and begins to sew some collars, her thoughts floating back to her days at Moses' just after the first war, when the girls would talk about their men friends and whether there would be any sausages left in the butcher's by Saturday. They'd recite the Moses poem.

The Lord said unto Moses
All Jews shall have Long Noses
Excepting Aaron and he shall have a Square 'Un.

Then they'd moan about the heat in the pressing room and how you couldn't get a bar of Watson's soap for love nor anything else. And most of all they would talk about their families.

Can't you get off that machine for a single minute? He slams his paper on the table. Morning, noon and bloody night. The sound's enough to drive a man round the twist.

Well how do you expect us to pay our way? she says, startled by her vehemence. It's not like I see much of the money you're making.

Before the sentence is out of her mouth, he is round the table.

Grabbing the flesh of her upper arm he begins to shake her like a pepper pot, so hard her head feels as though it might tumble to the ground.

You bleedn . . . he struggles for the word and, failing to reach it, thumps his fist down on the table.

I ain't done nothing, it ain't my fault, she sobs.

But he is reaching for her with all his anger now. A sour, blackening cloud wraps around the house, bearing fists of rain, each punch rolling like thunder in her bones. After he is done, he leaves her on the floor, with bruises blooming on her sallow skin.

The rest of the day she sews and sews. By six her hands have swollen up like boxing gloves. She goes to bed thinking about the wives in *Titbits* and *Reveille* and wondering where and why she went so badly wrong.

The following morning her teeth lie in icy slush in their jam jar. Upstairs the lodger belches and heaves himself from his bed. She reaches for the pot of Melrose on the dresser and rubs some into her toes for the chilblains, wonders how it would do for bruises. Then she dresses, puts the copper on to boil and goes out to the privy to feed the chickens. The sky is brittle grey and even though no bombs have fallen that night, the breeze gives off its habitual smell of cordite.

Somewhere west of the High Street a bit of sun has muscled out from behind the cloud cover and is glinting off a barrage balloon. She pulls at the door of the privy but it does not give way so she pulls a little harder, feels the ice crack and the metal suddenly springing back. The birds chuck and pout. She pours the contents of the feed bucket – potato peelings and old tea mostly – on to the hard ground and seats herself on the toilet.

Back in the house, Len is stuck, head first, in the newspaper. She makes a pot of tea.

Ain't you having breakfast? he asks.

Only one rasher left, she says.

Oh. His voice sounds almost contrite.

I'll go and fetch half a loaf later on, she says.

She is woken that night by the sound of Len pulling the string up through the letterbox outside and diving for the key. She hears the lock click open then another man's voice, soft but urgent, followed by Len, repeating something in an insistent tone. The two men remain in the kitchen for a long while before Len opens the door into the front room and lands on the bed.

'Ere, she whispers, but he is already asleep, his long arms with their fighter's fists stretched out over the pillow and away from her. She feels his breath dewy on her hair, his body pillowy beside her, his toes curling and uncurling the sheet.

She knows then that some kind of rip has opened in Len's heart but he will never let her in to sew it up again.

On 7 December 1941 America joined the war.

One Saturday just after the Yank invasion, Dora appears on the doorstep at Altmore Avenue with a smile on her face and a jaunty look.

Last night a Yank ship come in down the Royals, Jen. You want to take a peek?

They take off down the Barking Road towards Silvertown, the grey sky slung like a blanket overhead, pausing for a moment at Custom House to catch their breath. The Thames is at low tide, the water shrunk back thirty feet on either side, leaving its coughed up bomb debris on the smear of foreshore. A lighter is moored up by the Albert Dock Basin and three men are unloading sacks from the hold on to the quay with dockers' hooks. The smell of the foreshore mud travels by them, then a gummy smell followed by the reek of cooked yeast from Truman's brewery. There are other smells too: the stench of animal render from Knight's Soap, creosote from the tar pits, gasoline from the oil depot and liquor from the sugar refinery. All of this great East End stink is rising up on the westerlies and making its way towards the English Channel.

The two women pick their way through a pile of sandbags and descend into North Woolwich Road. Silvertown pours out in front of them, the damp black terraces and disreputable pubs and common little shops dwarfed by ships. A clean-up detail is working on a dusty gape where a building once stood.

To their left looms the Victoria Dock, to their right the Royal Albert and in each, poking above the brick massif of the dock wall, sit two huge Naval vessels, protected by looped coils of barbed wire and sandbags. They walk towards the crumbled remnants of Union Mills, remembering its demise a few years before, which had sent out clouds of white flour across the East End. Thinking there had been a gas attack, men and women had donned their masks and scattered across the streets like rats before terriers. By the following morning the flour was piled up in greyish mounds around the corners of nearby buildings and the streets were full of ragged women trying to scoop what was left into potato sacks.

Oh they got another one in, says Dora. Ain't it grand, though?

They pass a boy leaning against the sandbags at the bus stop clutching the bundle of morning papers he has not managed to sell.

You know how long the Yank boats are in? Dora asks him.

Might do for tuppence.

She inspects his face, filthy from the newsprint, then takes two pennies from her purse.

Till the high tide.

Well ain't you arrow-sharp now, boy? Which high tide?

The boy shrugs, picks up his newspapers and bowls off down the road before disappearing up an alley running alongside Johnson's Paint Factory, the coins clamped in his fist.

Poor Silvertown, sighs Dora. It never was much and now it's less. Look at the place. Filthy! But you know what my old man says, Jenny?

Nah, what?

My old man says there ain't no filth you can't plant potaters in.

CHAPTER 13

On one particular day sometime in the middle of the last winter of the war, something unexpected happens. The day begins as it always does, at six. Jenny rises, alone (she is almost always alone now), puts on the kettle, makes herself a cup of tea and takes breakfast with the bomb-outs lodging in the upstairs rooms. After breakfast she whitens the steps and washes the windows and scrubs the lino and at eight, as usual, she begins work on the collars. At one o'clock or thereabouts she eats a sandwich made with half a tinned sardine then sits back down to the Singer. At six she has brown soup, being careful to make enough for Len, who does not return to eat it. At nine-thirty she puts on a kettle for her last cup of tea, reads a story in an old copy of *Reveille*, and begins the preparations for bed. In these respects her day is like every other day. Sleep slinks up, knocking her sideways for a while. Sometime in the middle of the night she wakes and, feeling her way across the kitchen lino, reaches for the torch and steps outside. The air is as cold as a copper's boot. She opens the door to the privy, shuts it quickly and turns to sit, accompanied now by the disgruntled murmurs of the chickens. Her head aches from the frosty air and underneath her bedsocks purple chilblains stir. She directs her torch to the strips of newspaper beside the toilet and begins to cast her eye over the snippets of war news and dog results.

Back inside the house, she notices the tin bath is missing from its hook. Her curiosity roused, she goes into the bedroom and checks beneath and above the bed, then tramps softly up the stairs to the lodgers' rooms. The bedroom doors open to reveal a few sleeping bodies and a great deal of mess but no tin bath. She creeps back down the stairs and remembers the understairs cupboard. She opens the door and there she finds it. The tub. And inside the tub, a body. But whose? Her first thought is to rush upstairs and wake the lodgers, but on a moment's consideration she changes her mind. She finds herself wondering what one of the wives in the *Reveille* stories would do in such a situation. A dead body in the bath, not her husband's (somehow she is sure of that), but very likely something to do with him. And Len nowhere to be seen. She has visions of policemen and nosy neighbours and a shaming paragraph in the newspaper. Another thought rushes in. Supposing the body is a German *and Len has killed him*. Quite a different picture comes to mind. She has visions of local dignitaries and medals and the hushed respect of the neighbours. A German! It strikes her that she doesn't really know what a German might look like. There was Utz the butcher, of course, but he spoke English so he couldn't have been a bona fide foreigner. In the tub is a real enemy German of the sort who eat babies. She directs the torch to the form in the bath and daring herself to look sees a pig. A large, dead pig.

The next morning the pig has gone, the only reminder a thin, brown stain on the lino. The lodgers come down to breakfast bleary-eyed. She sizes them up over their slices.

Any of you see Len last night? An array of shaking heads.

She passes the day in a kind of torture, imagining thick streaky bacon, the fat as soft as marshmallow, or a stew of belly pork with a few carrots and some leeks thrown in. She goes to bed rumbling and falls asleep to the sound of bready sausages sizzling in a pan somewhere in the hungry space behind her eyes. The next morning she wakes up to a remembered smell of gammon steak and roast pork, all juicy crackling and tender fat. She goes through the day imagining ham with parsley sauce, followed by a thick chop with the kidney still attached and the rind all syrupy, a chewy trotter, some chitterlings fried to curling, or a slab of moist liver done in onion gravy.

Sometime in the afternoon, the sound of the doorbell brings her to. She shuffles through the hallway, rubbing her sore hands. Outside on the step are two coppers, a thin, dark, self-righteous-looking man and a taller man with dusk-coloured hair and ginger whiskers.

Oh lord, she thinks, it's the pig.

The dark one says hello and explains that they are on a routine visit.

Not yer usual, though, says Jenny.

Pardon us? says the dark one.

Routine, she says.

Oh no, says the ginger man, looking relieved, I suppose not.

What's up? Jenny tries to hide a tic that has started up in her eye.

It's nothing urgent, Mrs Page, says the ginger one, nothing urgent at all. We're just popping by for a nice chat.

Well, you'll have to come back, she says, a little too defensively. I'm here on me own.

Appreciate that Mrs Page, the ginger one smiles back. The two policemen don't move. She glances up the road to make sure Mrs MacReady isn't twitching curtains.

Mind if we come in for a minute?

The dark one is already in the hallway. Mind if he just has a quick look around?

The ginger one says, I could murder a cup of tea.

While putting on the water she scrambles around for an explanation for the pig.

Terrible business this war, says the dark one. Never thought we'd see the like. Still, you do what you can, your patriotic duty, like. He is seated now, with his helmet resting on the table beside.

A very tidy place, if I may say so, Mrs Page, continues the ginger one, peering out of the kitchen window. Lots of space to store things. Husband fond of the dogs, I hear.

She brings the pot of tea to the table, says nothing. The dark one stirs his and tests it.

Is it just the dogs he likes, Mrs Page, or is Mr Page partial to the beasts of the field or the farmyard, say?

He's fond of canary birds, she says, if that's what you mean.

The coppers swap glances and sideways grins. She detects a flash of something. The dark one makes a slurping noise with his tea.

He do come home with a rabbit from time to time, she continues.

A rabbit? says the dark one, nodding. Skinny thing a rabbit is. Not much meat on a rabbit. More meat on a pig than a rabbit.

Don't see many of them around nowadays, says Jenny. Except in the pig clubs, of course.

The dark one makes a gobbling noise in his tea.

Not so many in the pig clubs neither, Mrs Page. You wouldn't believe it but there's all kinds of pigs going astray from the pig clubs. Amazing how many of them pigs just disappear. You'd think they'd be located wandering the streets eventually. It's a bit of a mystery. He sighs and replaces the helmet, stands ready to leave. Well, we won't keep you from your work.

In the summer of that year, 1944, as the war is looking winnable, the busmen go on strike and the Home Guard are sent in to help out. In the first days of the strike, Len occupies himself counting his boxes of bully beef and tea, making endless little notes and calculations in his book and going about his ARP duties. As the strikes go on and the summer moves into autumn, he talks less and less of his busman's duties and more and more of quitting the buses altogether.

The newspapers begin to accuse the strikers of a lack of patriotism. Whatever the busmen's conditions, whatever their rates of pay, they say, the facts are that there is a war on and there are men out on the front risking their lives. Slowly at first, then in a flood, the Pages' neighbours bypass number 27. Men and women they've known for years fail to acknowledge them on the street. Even Paterson the butcher is frosty. Len returns home from the ARP in terrible rages. To be accused of unpatriotic feelings! He, who gave up the best years of his youth to serve his country in the festering jungles of the Orient. The best years of his youth! He, who endured malarial fever and blackened moods. To be accused, a decade on, of a lack of patriotic pride. He wears the injustice of it like a lead belt.

Finally, he can take no more. At the age of forty-one, Len Page hands in his notice, quits the buses and strikes out for himself. There are bargains to be had among the ruins of the East End and Len means to take advantage of them. With the money he has made from smuggling bully beef and tea he puts down a deposit for the lease of a small corner shop on a wide road beside bridges, docks and factories, an area which is at the moment devastated by years of bombing but he is sure as any man can be it is an area with a sparkling future. An often forgotten slub of land just east of the River Lea in the shadow of the Royal Docks through which, all during the war, he has driven his buses. He likes the name of the place. Silvertown.

He intends to modest a café for the transport workers passing through the docks. He will call it The Cosy Corner after the tiny shop and post office in Upminster that sat among the reeds and windy fields of his beloved childhood home.

CHAPTER 14

There never was any silver in Silvertown. Smoketown, Sulphurtown, Sugartown – the place could have been called any of those things and no one would have blinked.

A thousand years ago, the land between the Lea and Roding rivers – a stretch of five miles or so bounded to the south by the Thames and to the north by the old Roman track that is now the Barking Road – was fetid and empty marsh. It was known as Hamme and belonged to Guthrum the Dane who had won it in battle against King Alfred in 878. What Guthrum did with Hamme is not recorded – most likely nothing, since the area was pocked with quicksand pits and subject to almost constant flooding. Gradually Hamme fell back into the hands of the Saxons. In 1066 William the Conqueror passed through on his way from Hastings to Barking Abbey, where he held court while waiting for the Tower of London to be completed. In some fields on the banks of the Roding, William met a deputation from Edgar Atheling, the Saxon heir to the throne. From then on the fields became known as the Parly Marshes.

The area changed very little for centuries. Ships from Continental Europe would sail up the Thames and into the Lea and discharge their passengers at Stratford where there was a bridge and a road, but the marshes were left to themselves. The transformation of the area came in the middle of the fourteenth century when Edward

III, concerned for the health of Londoners, ordered that cattle should come no closer to the city than the Lea River. An abattoir was quickly built in Stratford and slaughtering became the Lea's first industry.

The riverine strip passed to Haimo, the Sheriff of Kent, who renamed it Wicklands, from the Anglo-Saxon word Zwischenland meaning Between Lands. The strip stretched from Bugsby's Reach, south of present-day Canning Town in the west, to Gallions Reach in the east. It was remote, marshy and increasingly surrounded by slaughterhouses, tanneries and dye works. Four hundred years later, it was still a hellish place. Sir Allan Apsley stationed his sailors there in the war against the Dutch in 1667 and wrote in his diaries that so many of his men came down with 'fevers and agues' that they 'cannot be persuaded that they are obliged to stay'. A century and a half later, in 1828, a philanthropist by the name of Mills spent £10,000 on an orphan boys' settlement at the western edge of the area. The settlement was designed to teach the boys of East London the craft of brickmaking. But in spite of their destitute state, the orphan boys ran away.

The eastern edge of what is now Silvertown had problems of its own. From the thirteenth century onwards, London's fish supplies had been unloaded at Barking Creek, where the Roding empties into the Thames. Many of the city's fishermen and jobbing sailors lived at East Ham and by the seventeenth century a thriving smuggling industry had begun there, the smacks bringing tobacco and spirits up Barking Creek and landing them on the empty marshes. Where there was drink and tobacco there was of course fighting and gambling, the two happily converging in bare knuckle fights which were held in a makeshift ring dug from the bog below East Ham Church. The Church graveyard was lonely and there was at that time a profit to be made in selling dead bodies and by the mid-1800s bodysnatching from East Ham Church had reached such a pitch that relatives of the dead had to pay for nightwatchmen to stand guard over their loved ones' bodies until nature had rendered them useless to medics and anatomists. Deprived of the dead, the snatchers turned to the living. Press gangs regularly swept through the area, packing their unfortunate victims into the smuggling smacks and ferrying them out to ships waiting for them at sea.

The marshes south of the Barking Road and to the west of East Ham remained remote and impenetrable. In 1800 only one house stood between the Bow and Barking Creeks on the banks of Gallions Reach. This building, known as the Devil's House, was then owned by the Ismay French family. History does not record what the Ismay Frenches were doing there, but by 1820 the Devil had evicted them and the abandoned house became the home of stray dogs and the occasional marshman trapped in an unexpected fog while tending his cattle and unable to get back home.

The marshland would have remained an unregarded stretch of reedbeds had it not been for George Bidder. Bidder was working in George Stephenson's railway business as an accountant. In the 1840s, Stephenson won a contract to work on a new stretch of railway across the marshes with a station at North Woolwich to link to the ferry that crossed the Thames there. Bidder spotted an opportunity and bought all the land between Bow Creek and Gallions Reach. By then there were three houses and a single road, the remains of an old Roman track called Prince Regent Lane. It was an inauspicious spot. The marsh was seven feet below the high tide mark and in the spring the entire area was flooded. Bidder named his purchase Land's End.

Though the land itself was unprepossessing, it was close enough to London to be of interest to C. J. Mare, who bought a few acres from Bidder on the western edge at Orchard Yard and set up an ironworks and ship-building business. Fifty years later, Thames Ironworks, as the business became known, had built eight hundred and thirty vessels and was responsible for the construction of Blackfriars and Hammersmith Bridges. Its football team went on to become West Ham Football Club. And, of course, my great grandfather, Frenchie Fulcher, was employed there for a time.

While Mare was moving into Orchard Yard, another entrepreneur named Hall bought some acres to the east. Hall's purchase proved an even better one than Mare's. In the 1850s the St Katharine's Dock Company bought the adjoining land, sunk supports into the marsh and dug out what became the Royal Victoria Dock. (The skeleton of a whale and a 27ft long canoe were found among the diggings, which were then sent upstream in barges and used to fill in marshland to make Battersea Park.) The Vic was the first dock in the world to be built for iron steamships, the first to use hydraulic cranes for raising ships into the pontoon dock, the first to contain a refrigerated meat store. It made its owners a tidy profit within a year of its opening in 1855.

Four years earlier, in 1851, the Howard Brothers had set up the first factory in what was then still called Land's End. A year after *that*, S. W. Silver moved his waterproofing works from Greenwich to land adjacent to Howards', and when the brothers' business failed, Silver took it over. Silver's India Rubber and Gutta Percha factory flourished, and the area that had been first a part of Hamme, then a part of Wicklands and then Land's End, became known as Silvertown.

By 1900 Silver's was turning out 600,000 footballs a year, along with children's rubber balls (modelled on those Columbus had come across in Haiti), rubber shoes and Mackintoshes, the 'Silvertown' golf ball, ebonite (a kind of vulcanised rubber), pens, thimbles, beer stoppers, oboes and clarinets, rubber washers and tyres, tubing for vinegar manufacture and photographic developing trays. Around the same time, Silver's were laying telegraph cables across the world from snub-nosed cable ships. They laid cable between Key West and Havana, through the West Indies to Panama, from Algiers to Marseilles and from the Cornish Lizard to Bilbao.

But there were still no roads in the southern stretch of Silvertown and the only way to reach Mr Silver's works was to walk along the river wall or draw up in a boat.

In the mid-1850s Hall began laying out cheap terraces on the sticky substrate on the northern side of the Dock between Tidal Basin and Custom House to serve as lodgings for the navvies digging out the Vic dock, and modestly called the place Hallsville. Houses were run up for £80 a piece, their only drains the marsh dykes which were themselves now cut off from the river by the Victoria Docks. By the time my grandmother was born, Hallsville had melted into Canning Town, itself the entrepreneurial invention of, yes, a man called Canning. Hall's grandiosity was misplaced. The area had rapidly become notorious. 'There is a suburb,' wrote Charles Dickens in 1859, 'which is quite cut off from the comforts of the Metropolitan Buildings Act; therefore is chosen as a place of refuge for offensive trade establishments turned out of town; those of the oil boilers, gut-spinners, varnish-makers, printers' ink makers and the like. Cut off from the support of the Local Managing Act, this outskirt is free to possess new streets of houses without drains, roads, gas or pavement.' Sewage sat behind the houses in pools, waiting for a flood tide to carry it away. When the flood tides came, Hallsville and Silvertown were drenched in floating sewage and their roads were impassable. The local doctor had to wear seaboots to make his rounds. There were about 5,000 living in Silvertown then, and many more in Hallsville.

Dickens had spotted something about the area no one else had noticed. Ever since Edward III had banned cattle from crossing the Lea westwards into London, the river had become a boundary between Middlesex and the Essex marshlands. Industry and housing to the east of the Lea being less regulated, the river had developed into a kind of Styx, separating the relative order of inner London from an unclean zone beyond. East of the Lea, noxious industries sprang up; factories burned rubber and crushed bones and sank pitch lakes; tanners leaked lime and arsenic; sugar was refined there using boiling ox blood. For centuries men and women had collected human shit on the banks of the Lea for the alum that was in it. Charles II put a stop to that because his beer was made with Lea water, but thereafter the shit simply gathered in stinking clumps and joined the other debris which collected in the bend of the Thames where it broke into Bow Creek. Huge mounds of old timber, scraps of metal, bricks, rotting paper and the drowned bodies of dogs piled into sludgy hills to be picked over by muddy-coloured gulls and the city's destitute. At Barking Creek Marc Bazalgette's Northern Outfall Sewer flowed out into the Thames. Built in 1863 with three channels each 9ft in diameter, the sewer poured the whole of North London's sewage directly into the river water. This was where the victims of the sinking of the Princess Alice drowned. Twenty-five years later, possibly as a response to those awful deaths, a clarifying works was built at the mouth of the sewer but you could still smell Barking Creek for miles around.

Human debris washed up there, too. For as long as anyone could remember the enclaves around the Lea heaved with abandoned sailors, with exiles and the spoils of forgotten wars and religious persecutions. Huguenots arrived, Irish came during the famine, Jews after the pogroms. The place was a refuge of sorts. Black men could camp out at the cheap boarding houses of Chequerboard Alley in Canning Town with their white wives without being hounded.

Indians frequented the Coloured Men's Missions. The Chinese set up small businesses. And the rural poor, edged off their land, came to Silvertown seeking work around the docks.

The arrival of the Beckton Gasworks brought some temporary prosperity to the area. A few years after Silver set up, the Gas Light and Coke Co. began work on the construction of the largest gasworks in the world beside the Barking Creek. The spot was renamed Beckton after Simon Adams Beck who ran the company. Gas caught on slowly. The first gas light was turned on in Pall Mall in 1809, frightening a wary public who imagined that the lights would explode or burn up all the air, but by 1900 the Beckton Gasworks was supplying twenty per cent of the UK's gas and had absorbed many of those workers who had arrived in the area to dig out the Vic dock. Since there was no accommodation at Beckton, a special railway was built across the marshes to transport workers in from Canning Town. The work was terrible – for ten hours the retort workers shovelled coal into furnaces white with heat – and the pay was poor, but the workers unionised under Will Thorne and their miserable situation gradually improved.

In 1880 a sister dock to the Vic, the Royal Albert, was built, and by the turn of the century work had begun on a third dock, the King George V, which was to be scooped out of land to the south of the Albert. The First World War halted construction on the new dock for a while but when the KGV finally opened a month or two after Jenny Page's eighteenth birthday, the Royal Docks at Silvertown – the Vic, the Albert, and the KGV – together made up the largest area of impounded dock water in the world.

Factories shot up as fast as weeds. In 1876, Tate's sugar works moved into the area from Liverpool, hoping to exploit a new patent on cube sugar which Tate thought would go down better in London than in the north of England. Tate's still sits on the same site as it did then, a jumble of tubes and smoking chimneys and brick and breeze-block extensions making up what is the largest sugar refinery in the world. Encouraged by Tate's success, Abram Lyle moved his Greenock factory to Silvertown in 1881 from where he cranked out millions of tins of golden syrup. James Keiller and Son, manufacturers of marmalade, cocoa and jam, moved nearby, encouraged by the proximity of their raw product. Later, sweet manufacturer Trebor joined them, and sweet pickle makers Crosse and Blackwell took over Keiller's in 1920.

The sweet smells of Silvertown mixed with others more noxious. Odam's Chemical Manure Works went up on marshland next to Silver's. The land had originally been used by the royal butcher, Hudson, to graze his cattle. After rinderpest came into England from imported cattle, Hudson won the exclusive right to land and slaughter all imported cattle at Silvertown, where they could more easily be inspected and from whose bones and offal Mr Odam built up a tidy nitrate and phosphate business. Next door to Odam's, Burt, Boulton and Haywood dug a pitch lake to serve their coal tar business. On the other side of the lake, Spencer, Chapman and Messel spewed out commercial sulphuric acid, and just a little down the road, John Knight rendered animal by-products into Knight's Castille soap and sold the glycerine produced in the process of saponification to a local factory for the manufacture of nitroglycerine and dynamite.

Unlike other parts of London, which spread in a wayward, organic, deranged fashion, Silvertown came to maturity suddenly and shockingly in the shadow of the immense city to its west. In the space of fifty years a mix of Victorian entrepreneurs, chancers, opportunists, profitseekers, visionaries, bondsmen and capitalists turned the marshes, which had for hundreds of years been the haunt of mooches, vagrants and whatever scum the tide brought in, into a slick of warehouses, transit sheds, railways, factories, chemical works, processing plants, colliers, ship builders, roads, bridges, houses, pubs, seamen's missions, pawnbrokers, currency changers, social clubs, factory sports grounds, brothels, shebeens and cafés. There was as a consequence a fragile and almost desperate quality to the place, which was not and could not be disguised by any amount of sprucing or ornamentation. Wicklands was as Haimo described it, neither one thing nor the other, a little patch of Hades separated from the city by the River Lea.

Len Page cared nothing for Silvertown's past. What drew him to the place was its future. By the time he got there, the Royal Docks were the busiest section of the world's largest port and a thriving industrial hub, and they had every prospect of expanding. Two hundred and fifty thousand people lived or worked in and around the Royals. Thousands more came in on the tides, every one of them in possession of a mouth, a stomach and an appetite. And the future would bring yet more. *That* was what brought Len Page to Silvertown.

Shortly after Len announces his plans, he and Jenny take the number 101 bus to Silvertown to inspect their new premises. On the bus Jenny considers her future, once stable and respectable, now uncertain. Len has never witnessed first-hand the fickleness of the docks. But she has. She recalls the savage uncertainty of the shape-up and the long years of unemployment and the strikes and stoppages. These are the thoughts going through her head but she can do nothing about them, of course, because her thoughts are of little consequence to Len Page and his plans.

A long line of lorries makes its way from the dock gates, loaded with cargo. Beside them a group of factory girls are laughing and exchanging insults with some dockers. Len and Jenny stop at Gate

8. In his sentry box a PLA policeman looks on, nods politely and half-smiles.

Morning, says Len.

Morning, says the policeman.

From the other side of the dock wall a lorry pulls up and the driver's mate, a shabby boy too young for war, clambers out with a pile of customs forms. Taking advantage of this small distraction, Len casually pulls a pack of Lucky Strikes from the pocket of his jacket and offers one to the copper.

Take the pack.

The policeman's eyes strafe the tiny territory of the gate and, finding it all clear, he stuffs the pack inside his jacket. A thin smile toys momentarily on his lips.

Mind if I show the wife around?

Not done, sir, as a rule. Guvnor don't like it.

The policeman takes a draw on his cigarette and looks about.

What the guvnor don't see, says Len, his hand lingering delicately but insistently over his pocket, the guvnor don't need to worry about.

The policeman throws him a cagey look, as though conscious of being in the presence of some superior force.

Keep close to the gate then, and don't touch nothing. Anyone stops yer, say I authorised it.

Len and Jenny pass alongside the sentry box underneath a red-brick archway then out on to the quayside. Before them lies the stone grey water of Victoria Dock, and beyond that the swing bridge then the long black slur of the Royal Albert. On each side of the quay, away from the water, sit lines of warehouses and transit sheds. The southern quay where they are standing is almost wholly given over to grain stores, holding wheat, oats, barley, rye and maize, from the great agri-plains of America and Canada. Two ships are being unloaded at Pontoon Dock, their cargo swinging over on to the shore in great nets to be barrowed off at the quayside to Millennium Mills or the Premier Flour Mills or the Cooperative Wholesale Society grain store.

Beyond these an empty berth leads up to the swing bridge and the giant refrigerated warehouses standing along the north side of the Albert. In peacetime, these warehouses will hold three-quarters of a million lamb carcasses, tons of Argentinian, Uruguayan and Brazilian beef, mutton from Australia and New Zealand, American and Danish bacon, oranges from Morocco, Spain, bananas from the West Indies, Egyptian dates and Greek sultanas. Now they are half empty. Opposite them, on the south bank of the Albert, stretch the grey concrete quays of the KGV, dotted on the northern side with tobacco sheds, which even in wartime hold more tobacco than any other single place in the world: seven hundred and fifty thousand tons of best pressed leaf from the Carolinas and Virginia along with bales of shag from the West Indies and British Guiana. Country Life, Capstans, St Julien, British Oak Shag, Adkins Nut Brown – all have their stores here. A tobacco-built city it is, reeking of tar and resin, known to the locals simply as Tobacco Road, E16.

At the far end of the Albert and the KGV another cargo vessel comes and goes. As a very young woman, Jenny would walk down to the Connaught Bridge dividing the Victoria from the Albert and watch the passenger liners from the colonies, protectorates and possessions of the Empire discharge their cargo of men and women. Occasionally, very occasionally, she would imagine herself on one of those ships, the ships whose names were the markers of her childhood: Port Vindex, Patonga, Uruguay Star, Leeds City.

Today the quayside is lined with supply vessels, funnels in camouflage colours. A couple of small gunboats tug gently at their moorings. Between the spaces necklaces of lighters move, pulled by snub-nosed tugs. Hundreds of men shift about on the ships, in the lighters and on the quay, hooks in hand or swinging from their belts, barrowing sacks, chests, boxes from quayside to warehouse, catching the loads as they swing from the dockside cranes.

If this ain't the bloody business, whistles Len appreciatively. Largest port in the bleedn world.

But Jenny says nothing, remembering only the look on Frenchie's face when he came home from the shape-up empty-handed.

Know what drives the men what work in it? says Len, catching her eye and expecting an answer.

For a moment she glances at the men again. A kind of dizziness swells inside her head.

The buses?

Don't be so bleedn daft, he says. *Grub*, food, tucker, fodder, nosh. And that is what you and me are getting into, Jenny, 'cos that's what drives the men what work in the biggest bleedn port in the whole bleedn world.

Outside the dock in Silvertown, the factory girls are still standing at the bus stop on the Canning Town side of Silvertown Way, idly playing cats cradle. Len winks at them and they giggle back. The landscape of Silvertown is all lines. Factories, chimneys, lines of workers, buses, bus queues, the slabs of the docks, the neat grids of terraces, queues of traffic, children tethered to washing lines to keep them from going under the wheels, the ships anchored just off the fairwater, awaiting entry to the port, and the river slicing through it all. The lines serve to disguise what is actually a terrible casualness. Abandoned sailors, discarded men and women, lost children and a zig-zag of lives ruined by drink. They walk back up Silvertown Way, to a parade of modest shops just south of Dock Gate 8, passing a small and partly demolished grocers, next to that a bomb crater, then Jimmy Doherty's shoes which has a cheerful wooden sign outside in the shape of a boot. Next door to the shoe shop is the post office, followed by a little newsagent's displaying racks of this and that, then Patisson's grocer and just before the corner, Gladys Hobbs hardware, a clutter of galvanised buckets, mess-headed mops and coal scuttles threatening to tumble out on to the pavement.

Len stops in front of the corner shop, a small, nondescript building with a glass and cast-iron frontage that has long since gone dark with brick dust and grime. A baby blue door with an old-fashioned lock leads into a murky space beyond. He stands before it, an ordinary man with extraordinary ambitions and nearly half a century of plans. He catches her eye and smiles.

Welcome, he says, to The Cosy Corner Café. He thumps on the door and winks. Proprietor Leonard Stanley Page.

CHAPTER 15

It takes Len and Jenny a week to clean The Cosy Corner. For ten hours a day they sweep and swab and scrub. They clean until their backs feel broken and their skin shrivels from exposure to carbolic. In the midst of it all, a malarial fever chases through Len's body like a rabid dog, but he works on. Equipment turns up at odd, irregular hours: a gas oven, nearly new, a rickety butcher's table, a fistful of forks, knives and spoons. Payments are made, hands are shaken and questions are not asked.

We'll get this ugly duckling looking like a regular swan, says Len, the sweat dripping from his neck and pooling on to the lino.

Every day a new batch of men show up, take a look around, make approving noises and occasionally offer advice before clearing off to the pub. For a week Len sails around, back-slapping, Sonny-Boying, winking his way into their affections. She has never seen him so proud and so fresh with possibility. Not even on his wedding day. Certainly not on his wedding day.

And so, after a quarter of a century, Jenny Page finally turns her last collar. This is harder than she has expected. Tailoring isn't just what she knows, it's what she *is*. For two and a half decades the soft ticking of the treadle has been her music and it is hard to imagine any kind of life without it. Her body has moulded itself to the machine. She has the right arm of a stevedore and the hands of an old woman. The calf on her treadle leg is twice the size of the other. Her fingers are clumped by arthritis and her eyes are weak and watery and find it hard to see anything that is not directly ahead. The trembles in her hands are a constant reminder of the motions of the needle.

Stitching's no life, says Dora, who got out of the tailoring trade after her first child and now works in a grocer's shop.

Well, it's been mine, says Jenny.

That's what I meant, pet, says Dora casually. Then, changing the subject, But, really, Jenny, what kind of a man goes and sets up a caff in the middle of a war in a place that's bombed to bits?

A Len kind of a man, I s'pose.

What kind of a fella sets up a caff when there ain't nothing to eat this side of America 'cept bread and marg?

The kind of man who keeps half a ton of pork on the trotter in the understairs cupboard and four hundred tins of bully beef on the floor and a flock of chickens in the privy, thinks Jenny, but says nothing. It would take too long to explain.

He reckons he'll do most of the cookin'.

My arse he will.

Now Dor, you know that ain't fair. Jenny adjusts the angle of her teeth and slops down the last of her tea. It really is pointless talking about what Len is or isn't likely to do because Len always does what he wants, regardless.

Well it's for the best, says Dora at last. Sorry to say, pet, but we both know you're a bloody awful cook.

By the following Saturday they are done. The décor is not what you might call perfect, nor impressive even, but in the circumstances it will do. Where the paint has peeled from dampened woodwork Len has patched it up in camouflage colours 'borrowed' from a cousin, who works in the paint shop at the Vic. They have polished

and cleaned the wooden booths and coated the table tops with ship's
varnish. The kitchen is kitted out by a friend of Len's in the scrapyard
business, the other bits and pieces salvaged from relatives, acquaint-
ances, men Len knows. When the last plate has been stashed, the
final wipe-over done, they stand back and admire. Len says, C'mon
girl, less go down Tate's for a bit of a knees-up.

He leads them downhill, swiping the sweat from his face and
cursing softly. They walk hunched against the rain towards the quiet
of the river. The moon is thin tonight and obscured by clouds and
they can barely see the water but they can hear it, clapping softly
against the jetty pilings.

Seems almost peaceful now, says Jenny.

Seems that way I'll grant yer, Len says, wiping sweat. But it
ain't. Ain't no peace any place.

No, I don't s'pose there ever is, she says.

Their eyes drift out to meet the long liquid stripe in the solid
spill of the city, with the moon above, pulling the water eastwards
towards the place from where all the trouble has come. Sensing the
distance between them now, they turn and carry on, across the
brow of Silvertown towards Tate's. Jenny is thinking of Frenchie,
dead from rage and disappointment and too many nights in the pub.
She can see him as clearly as though he were standing right in front
of them, nailing planks, sanding off and varnishing the boats at
Orchard Yard, boats that would sail to faraway places Frenchie
would never see. A memory surfaces. She is opening the door and
finding him sitting on his own, staring into the middle distance,
smoke curling from the cigarette in his lips. Just sitting. And the
next day the same, as though someone had emptied him out and
put him away for safekeeping.

Tate's social club is full of women dressed in their threadbare
imitations of finery and men in uniforms. Len waves to a giant man

with black greased hair and a balding patch who is sitting at the bar nursing a drink beside a bored-looking blonde. They're both drunk, but he is holding it better than she is. Off to one side a gramophone is playing an Edmundo Ros number, or something like it, and a few couples are dancing tentatively. The man waves back and holds out his palm and begins to write something on it with the index finger of his other hand. A little piece of men's business. Len nods back and smiles and calls the man a bastard under his breath. The giant returns to the blonde.

They walk over to a table and order a couple of drinks and are about to order a couple more when the giant appears from the shadows.

Lenny, me mate, what can I do for yer?

Nothin I can't do for meself, Freddie.

You going to introduce me to the lady?

Len stabs his cigarette in Jenny's direction. That's the missus.

The giant hesitates, wondering how far he can go and where he'll be when he gets there and decides to try it out.

The missus, he says, *another one*. And sticking out his hand, Well, pleased to meet you, Mrs Page, I really am.

For a moment Len sits, motionless, sucking on his cigarette.

What are you after Freddie? he says with an edge.

The giant feigns surprise. Me? Nothin', govnor, nothin' at all. How's that caff of yours? Mutual acquaintance tells me you's thinking of calling it The Cosy Corner. That's a bloody queer name, Len, if you don't mind me saying. He turns to Jenny, who had tucked herself into a corner. Wouldn't you say so, Mrs Page? Seems bloody queer to me in any case. The giant rolls up a sleeve, displaying the rump of muscle underneath. So when are you thinking to open 'The Cosy Corner', Lenny? Only we keep hearing one day it's in a fortnight, the next day it's a week after. We thought mebbe you'd run out of cash, Lenny, old mate.

Len leans back in his chair and takes a long, slow sip of his beer. I'll be sure to send you an invitation to the opening, Freddie.

I'll look forward to that, Lenny, I'll look forward to that very much.

They watch him slouch back to the blonde and a moment later the social club looks like a happy Saturday night once more, with men and women dancing and everyone having as good a time as can be had when the booze is short and the men are going back to the front. Shortly afterwards, someone starts up on a tatty piano and a woman in a brown dress which probably fit her snugly before the war but now hangs like a curtain sings 'We'll Meet Again' and all of a sudden it is as though the years have drifted away and they are sitting in a club on a regular Saturday night before the war when their hearts were less strained and their souls less bruised than they are today.

The only things missing are the children. How could Jenny have forgotten them, away now half their lives, the boy away most of his. She recalls the yearly visits, the two children stiff as rabbits in sight of a gun, and the two dour old hags allotted as their keepers smiling politely beside them. *Be nice to your mother. Ask your mother how it is in London now.* She remembers the sullen looks, the eyes that hold feelings she cannot reach.

The Cosy Corner Café's first day in business is a damp, foggy Monday in the late autumn of 1944. Business is slow. But the second day is a little better and the next day better still and gradually, The Cosy Corner begins to build a regular clientele.

Events in Silvertown prove good for business. The winter of 1944 turns out to be the coldest anyone can recall. There is another bus strike and in the spring of 1945 the dockers walk. Buses disappear off the streets, cargo piles up and men stand idly at picket lines longing for the comfort of a hot meal. The café is well positioned, right beside the entrance to Tate and Lyle's Plaistow Wharf and a minute from Gate 8 of the Royal Victoria Dock. More than that, working men like the atmosphere. The Cosy Corner is a scrap of homeliness in an unforgiving place. But there is another reason for its success too. And that is Len Page. He makes a fine liver and onion dinner. His mash is the best in Silvertown. The clientele appreciate his friendly manner, his wit and energy. But above all that, they sense that Len Page is a man who is going somewhere and won't stop until he gets there. A man to know.

By the spring Len is in expansive mood, the centre of his own bulging universe.

Wait till the war ends, Jenny, he says. Just wait.

They do not have to wait long, as it turns out. VE day arrives as an announcement on the wireless at Altmore Avenue.

Well, would you cocoa? laughs Len Page, opening the back door and letting his dogs into the kitchen. For some while now they have shared their yard with an assortment of greyhounds – convalescents mostly, and the odd bitch on heat – as a favour to Len's growing tribe of friends. It's all over. He grabs a brindle bitch and, rubbing her silky flanks, braces himself for her tongue. The bleedn war is bleedn over! He zooms towards Jenny and clamps her in his arms so hard she feels lightheaded and touched by some deeply buried feeling she thought she had lost.

Len, give over! I ain't one of your dogs.

He pulls away, grinning, and they stand rooted that way for a moment, with the flapping dogs doing circuits around them.

That night they go down to Tate's and it is late by the time they begin the walk home. Here and there, people have pulled aside their blackouts. The sky is white with flares. They pass by smiling men and laughing women, past bodies slumped drunk in the gutters.

For the first time in six years the city blares with sounds, tentative at first, then roaring. People are crying, shaking with the force of grief they have kept bottled for what seems like an eternity. No one is free from thoughts of the dead that night. It is as though the ghosts of Daisy, Ria, Tom and all the rest have sprung from the shadows and the living can at last hear their whispers.

A greying day in late autumn 1945 finds Jenny Page walking through Liverpool Street Station to wait for the 11.07 from Cambridgeshire. On that late morning, the station is airless and claustrophobic. Her chest tightens, from the engine smoke, or is it nerves? She makes her way to the same platform from where she had waved her children off, with a tight, unbelieving goodbye not thinking – how could you think – that it might be six years before they would be returned. The platform is crowded with women making noisy, excitable small talk.

A porter asks her if she's waiting for the St Ives train, then adds that second class will be alighting further down. He points to a distant part of the platform. You're free to wait anywhere you like, madam, of course, but you might find it more convenient at the other end.

She looks at him for a moment, nods and begins to wander along the platform, across the lines of wealthy mothers, nannies and plump grandmothers, to where the poor people stand, their clothes and faces scoured by war.

My grandparents hardly ever visited their evacuated children. In fact, I'm not sure that Len ever did. It was hard to find the time or the money to get up to St Ives, but that really wasn't it. Len and Jenny Page didn't want to go. Len had his own reasons. He was never so much interested in his children as in the products of their labour. He took after his own father in that respect. I'm tempted to think that Jenny's reasons were more complicated. I suspect she found it easier to cut herself off because staying in touch was too painful. It was not quite an abandonment, more a failure of nerve.

And so Jenny stands and waits and sucks on an Everton mint and feels apprehensive. The children she waved off were city kids: taut, wan little things with tough heads. And now, what? She wonders how they will cope. She wonders if she will have enough to give them. She wonders what to say. The porter passes her again, carrying a hat box. Won't be long now, he says. He flips the box over his shoulder and adjusts his cap. She watches him turn and shuffle along the platform to the first class area.

Her eyes begin to ache. She presses her palms against the lids, making patterns of red veins appear. It is a good feeling, being in that blind world behind the eyes.

Twenty minutes after its scheduled arrival, the train from St Ives draws slowly into the station before heaving to a standstill. Moments later, doors swing open. Squinting through the smoke, women fling themselves forward. There is the smell of the brakes, and children tumble to the platform. Children swinging bags and pulling up socks, children clanking conkers and stepping on each other's toes, every kind of child, pushing, laughing, bluff and bright in the moment. So many children it is hard not to feel swamped by them.

She peers unseeing through the haze. Then she spots them. Waddling through the smoke, the spindly girl reduced to a pale streak topped with luscious chestnut curls, the boy falling behind. They are dressed in clothes she'd made for them to come home in, without knowing what would fit. The little girl's coat trails in the dust and the boy's short trousers are so long he sweeps the spare fabric behind him like a train. She waves and the girl's face suddenly beams and she says something to her brother who, hanging back behind his sister, turns away as if to collect himself. Step by step they approach, these pieces of her heart closing in like beads of mercury, until they are right in front of her, not six feet away.

Hello, says Jenny.

The girl and the boy swap anxious looks. Eventually the girl says, The train stopped at St Albans and a man got on with a funny hat.

She wiggles under her coat, stealing glances at her mother's face. How thin she is. And pale. She looks like a sign post. Her voice has changed too, the East End scrubbed off her tongue. The boy begins to cry. Well, he is only eight or nine. (Which, she can't remember!) She reaches down and takes his wrist and the tears stop. If anything he looks surprised. He scrutinises her hand, running his eyes along the gnarls and bulbed fingers, then drops it.

There, there, she says. She leans towards him but he backs away a little. Are you hungry?

They gave us a sandwich but it was horrid, says the girl. She coughs low in her chest and swallows whatever comes up. We swapped it with a girl who had an egg but she started crying.

We'll go down the caff and get you a bit of tea. Remembering the bullseyes in her pocket, Jenny draws out the little bag and picks three sweets from the sticky mass in the bag.

They clamber on to the top deck of the bus, sucking on the bullseyes, and by the time they reach Shoreditch the three of them are reduced to a salivating, sweet-filled silence.

We usually walk, the girl says at last. Where we live we don't take the bus.

You live 'ere now.

The girl nods and stares out of the window.

Where you was living before was different, see? There wasn't so many holes to trip over.

No holes, repeats the girl.

Mind you, there wasn't so many holes here neither, before.

The girl says nothing. Before is half her life ago.

They march in single file from the bus stop, hit every now and then by a cold wind blasting from the alleyways, and reach the café just before the teatime rush. A couple of lorry men are sitting at one of the booths, drinking from chipped enamel. At the counter, Len looks up, sees his children, strobes around as though searching for a response, and finally allows himself a smile.

Come here you bleedn rascals.

The children shuffle forward, uncertain. From somewhere at the back comes the tinny bleat of a wireless. He takes their hands and without looking at their faces, marches them to the table where two men are sitting.

Here's me nippers. Say hello to yer uncle Red and yer uncle Hanny.

The boy stares wild-eyed at the two men. The girl begins pulling on her father's hand.

Give yer uncles a smile, Len says. Be nice to yer uncles.

The girl pulls back on the hand and shakes her head. The boy musters a thin grimace.

Good kid, says Uncle Hanny, patting the boy on his head. Jus got back from the evacuation I suppose? He leans in, grinning conspiratorially. Bet they spoiled you rotten, didn't they?

Rotten, says Len. He winks at his children. He watches them run back to their mother. In the kitchen, Jenny begins spreading a couple of slices of bread with marrow jam. Five minutes later, Len bounds in with a large parcel wrapped in newspaper.

Here. He slams the parcel on the table, opens up the paper. Nestling there amongst the demob news is a pyramid of rusty meat.

No bones? she says.

Nothing.

Gristle?

He shakes his head.

What is it what don't have no bones nor gristle? she asks.

He shrugs. Horse, dog, whale, bleedn Nazi, who cares? he says, turning his attention to the children standing nervously beside the wreckage of dirty plates. Runty little buggers, ain't they. Taking the boy by the chin he shakes him a little. Never mind. Soon feed 'em up.

They watch Len disappear back into the café.

It's bread and jam then.

Who's Uncle Hanny? says the girl, chewing on her bread. And who's Uncle Red?

For this Jenny has no answer because she has never set eyes on either of them before.

CHAPTER 16

Len Page opens the meat store, fetches a slab of ox liver and whacks it down on the cutting board. The press of his business, of his *businesses* (there seem to be new ones every week), has left him irritable and tightly wound. The girl can't bleedn read for a living, he says, pulling the veins and connective tissue from the liver. At this rate she'll turn into a dictionary. She'll 'ave ter bleedn graft, same as the rest of us.

I ain't saying she won't, says Jenny, chopping tripe in the opposite corner.

Business won't run on bleedn books, says Len, yanking out the bile ducts.

I ain't saying it will, says Jenny, slapping down more tripe.

Ah, don't you start, I got enough on me plate, says Len, scraping at a green patch. All I'm saying is, when the girl's not at school I want 'er workin 'ere. And the second she leaves school I want 'er working 'ere an' all.

By this stage in her life, the girl has other ideas. She'd like to stay on at school and take up teacher training. Pipe dreams according to Len. But the girl is stubborn. The boy is a mystery, too. Together they are one of those irritating jigsaw puzzles in which most of the major pieces are missing. The boy is younger and will be easier to mould. He senses the girl will be a battle.

Put a man off his dinner to have her standing there, boggling at her books. Len wipes the liver blood on a cloth. She unsettles him. Whenever he looks at her he is reminded of the fields, the flat reed beds, the marshes of his home. She is his long exile.

Take the kid up Rathbone Market and do some shopping or something, he says.

Jenny sighs and reaches for the girl's hand.

Come on then.

The girl looks down at her peeling shoes and bites her lip.

Can I take my bicycle? Soon after their return to London, Len bought his children each a second-hand bicycle. As Len figured at the time, it takes them only ten minutes to pedal from school in East Ham to The Cosy Café, so they can put more time in helping about the place, and in the long run a bicycle costs less than the bus.

Outside in the street, her mother says, Yer old dad don't like you messin' around with books.

But Mum . . .

They both know that the girl will continue to mess around with her books and her father will continue to hate her for it and Jenny will be caught between the two of them, each as stubborn as the other.

Everyone is pretty stirred up that first winter after the war. It is too little to say the war has changed lives. It has reinvented the idea of what a life can be. In those months after the war, strikes, marches and protests hit the streets of London. The rules change and in the East End the rules are always more important than the law. The rules are what you live by; the law is just something you have to get around. And no one knows more about the rules than Len. All through the early Forties he works his patch, building networks and contacts and making a name for himself. By the time the war ends he has the rules down pat. He begins to dress like a man who is going somewhere. He wears bespoke suits and is careful to be seen with the right men. He treats off-duty coppers to a round in the pub. He invests in his dogs. He buys a wristwatch and, finally, just after the war, the grandest prize of all.

One hazy Sunday morning Len rises early and, issuing orders to Jenny, goes out without drinking his tea. There being no questioning Len that doesn't end in a dirty whack from a white-knuckled hand, Jenny does what she is told, buttons the children into their only set of clothes, spits on a handkerchief to clean their faces and, finding a tin of corned beef in the cupboard above the kitchener, cuts a few rounds of sandwiches.

Half an hour later, Len is commanding his family to wait for him on the pavement outside while he fetches 'the surprise'. So there they stand, self-consciously avoiding the curious gazes of the neighbours, when turning into the top of the road comes a glossy black motor car and at the wheel, looking mighty pleased with himself, is Len.

Blimey, says Jenny.

A real motor car it is, as black and dazzling as a flat-cut coal. All the way up and down the street, neighbours begin to creep from their houses to stand on their steps and stare.

Well get in then, he says. I brung Harry from Upton Park, you remember. His missus June gets terrible travel sick so she'll go in the front.

Jenny leans down and peeps inside the back window. The man has his face turned away but the woman in the front is vaguely familiar. She thinks back and brings to mind the Christmas party at Upton Park and the honey blonde with her fondant fancy. The woman catches her eye, smiles and, holding up the hand of a baby in her lap, forces it into a wave.

Ah, says Len, that's their little girl.

For the first ten miles or so of the journey, Harry holds a paper bag to his mouth and makes heart-breaking retching sounds. Poised on the warm leather seat, slightly worn and with the stuffing drawn to the sides to leave lumped scoops for the thin flesh of her buttocks, Jenny Page watches the view. The girl sits next to her, stiff as a chimney rod, and the boy hovers restlessly on her knees. In the front the woman bounces her baby to sleep then touches up her lipstick.

The route to Southend takes them through Barking, Ilford, Dagen-ham – emerald-coloured suburbs with fresh air and spritely parades of shops. It is a different world out here, no rubble, very few craters or bombed out spaces. The trees are allowed to grow unchecked along the verge, the little houses have miniature front gardens from which tidy rows of plantings wave. The people seem plumper and slower. She watches the women pushing their perambulators along the pavements, undaunted by the distances between roads, or the formidable loneliness of their surroundings.

Fields begin to emerge from behind the rows of housing. A rooty aroma of toasted barley seeps in from outside.

Funny smell, says the honey blonde, gazing out of the window at the stippled trees and low hedges.

Good enough to fill yer lungs, ain't it? laughs Len, lighting a Senior Service. They slow at a junction, turn right, then continue along an arterial road running between fields. Just as they are picking up speed along the straight, a colossal bang detonates from the back of the car. For an instant Jenny looks at Harry and Harry looks back. Then, grabbing the children, they crash to the floor of the back seat, clutching their heads, remembering the Luftwaffe opening their hatches.

Daft buggers! shouts Len. That's a backfire!

The back seat passengers clamber back on to their seats, cautiously at first, and look about. Outside the same fields stretch into the distant horizon.

Len and the honey blonde are talking as though nothing at all unusual has happened. June is saying, 'Ere, Lenny, ain't this near where you come out shootin'?

Well yeah, Len is saying, I ain't never short of a rabbit out here. Get some nice tender rabbit round these parts. He tilts his head, waiting for a confirmation from his wife.

Eh, I said tender rabbit. You gone deaf?

Don't mind her, says June, with a smile, she's just admiring the view.

As a matter of fact, Jenny Page is not admiring the view. The view, such as it is, disgusts her. The sky is a sinister blue, the crimped hedges look like trenches and the broad empty sweeps of the fields strike her as heartless. Where are the shops, the crowds, the comforting smells of industry? A memory comes to mind of the ice on the well in Billericay, of the dewiness of the pre-dawn air and the odour of fertility. They overtake a slow-moving tractor and she thinks of Berry and his dinners and considers all the men and women like him, who have never watched the lighters drifting down the Thames or eaten pickled cockles on a Friday night outside the pictures or seen a Chinaman or a lascar. She shakes her head. No wonder old Jim Page got to London and flipped his lid. He discovered what he'd been missing.

The sun pours in at the windows and the outskirts of Southend begin to appear, neat bungalows scattered between ordered parades of shops and the odd pub. The sea rises into view at last and Len turns the motor towards the blue horizon. Driving along the seafront they pass theatres and picture houses and coconut shies, bathing huts tricked out in pastel paint, eel and pie stalls and lines of genteel hotels. The beaches are still covered in sandbags and tank traps, but the sea is radiant in the sunshine and everything feels happy. There are men on the promenade with their arms snaking about their women and grins on their faces, and beside them, laughing children.

They make their way towards the pier, hugging their sandwiches. Harold forks out sixpence for a cardboard hat with Kiss Me Quick written on the front, saying if you've come to have fun you might as well bleedn well have it. He points himself in the direction of his wife, who laughs and says how sweet he is, then turns away to look at a donkey swinging by. They eat their sandwiches in cheerful companionship and wash them down with a strong, sweet tea from a stall along the pier, then walking to the end of the pier they stand and stare out across the glittering sea. The adults fall into silent contemplation.

What's it like, Len, the world? asks June at last.

Savage, Len says dreamily. It's all just savagery, innit?

On the way back, they fork out sixpence to see a bearded lady sitting in a dark tent, who is not very convincing, and a pair of Siamese twins who set the boy off crying. The weather turns, briefly, and dumps a cloudful of rain on them and they shelter in the arcade with the other daytrippers, jostled into smiling rows, chattering like park birds and trying to keep back the memories of booming air and sirens and guns. Then the rain clears, leaving dark stains on the paving stones.

Where's Harry? asks Len, looking around, then at June. A weary tic passes between them, then something more elusive. Can't have gone far, the bugger. Want me to check the pubs, June?

S'pose you'll have to.

Len grows small against the matted sky. A thought drifts into Jenny's head and stays there. It is a thought about June and Len and the fact that Len asked June what she wanted.

While the men are gone June wants to ride on the rollercoaster but she is worried that it will ruin her hair.

Oh won't you lend me your scarf, Jen? I couldn't bear to mess up my do, see.

Ain't you gonna wait for Harry? says Jenny, unknotting the scarf.

In truth, Jenny is anxious that they have moved too far from the spot where Len left them and the two men will have trouble finding them again.

Why don't we jess see if they're back up at the top of the pier?

What, says June, give up our fun? 'Sides, Harry don't like nothing like this. Harry don't like nothing *fun*.

Well I'm with Harry, says Jenny. You can keep yer rollercoaster. Wild horses.

Oh Jen, you wet blanket, says June, pulling a sulky face. You see to the baby then. I'll just have to ask this gent if he minds me sitting with his party.

Can't I go, Mum? asks the boy.

Not likely.

And so it is settled. June clambers into the car and waves while it climbs to the first descent. Moments later, they watch the car rocking at the top of its metal mountain before it tips, and they lose sight of it.

An hour or so later they run into Len and Harry, happy as lords, singing some tuneless thing and smelling of drink and drowned secrets.

Less go 'ome, says Len.

Where the heart is, croaks Harry.

The motor starts on the fifteenth rotation. Jerking along the coastal road, they take a last look at the sky-blue sea before turning inland towards the familiar stained clouds and brackish smell of London. Harry is hit by persistent hiccups, but by the time they reach Romford he has dissolved onto the leather seat like the oil on a tanner's rag and is snoring softly with a smile on his face and a pulse drumming under his eye.

The puzzle remains as to where Len got the money to buy his first motor. The Page family was still living on the edge of poverty, the children threadbare and in boots that pinched. It was the only private motor vehicle in Altmore Avenue. Neighbours would run to their windows and tweak open their nets to see it pass. On the street, men would tip their hats and women would nod and smile or even wave. Children would follow it along the road. It was one more step in my grandfather's reinvention of himself.

This reinvention was not without its setbacks. The Pages are working in the café one Saturday morning. The first rush is over. A few factory workers have come off shift and are tucking into an early lunch of brown liver and onions with boiled potatoes. Someone is shouting for egg and chips. Before long, the walls of the cucumber green room will be troubled by the echoes of dockers, lorrymen, warehousemen, factory girls, lightermen, ship repairers, sailors, soap wrappers, sugar packers, mud skippers, rivermen, newspaper hawkers, stevedores, customs men, tally clerks, ship painters, union men, crane operators, hatchmen, corn porters, tugmen, tar pit workers, wharfsmen, cleaners, ropesmen, chandlers, barmaids and welders. But for now, it is about as peaceful as it gets.

The children have been sent outside to play on their bicycles. They'll be brought in again when there are plates to shift and washing up to be done. Various deliveries from the Goods Shed are arriving at the back door. The Goods Shed is a partially bombed and derelict warehouse near Plaistow Wharf which is currently serving as a contraband exchange. As smuggling operations go, it's all very civilised. The police wait until the Shed is empty before they raid it because they get a cut on everything sold there. Without the Goods

Shed the pubs and shops and cafés of Silvertown would have closed down years before. In any case, the café's yard is filling up with boxes, tubs and tins that have fallen off the backs of lorries and from the hatches of ships.

In the kitchen Jenny is making a bread pudding in time for the noon flurry and keeping her eye on what customers there are while Len and Uncles Hanny and Red struggle to get some boxes under cover before the rain starts again. Jenny is just finishing up the bread and is about to begin peeling the next batch of potatoes when a man in dockers' garb flings himself through the door, shaking his head and panting.

Mrs P?

Yes? She feels what used to be her heart tapping away in her chest. It ain't the coppers is it?

Coppers? The man frowns, starts shaking his head. Oh no, Mrs P, it's worse than that. The man's mouth continues to open and close but the words seem to be bouncing off her. Her head suddenly feels as light as a barrage balloon. She hears herself say, Rosie?

Are you getting me, Mrs P, he's saying. It's yer girl I'm talking about. Yer little girl.

CHAPTER 17

Your daughter? asks a nurse in a brown uniform. I am sorry.

The waiting room outside the ward where Jenny is sitting smells of carbolic and damp and cabbage. She has been sitting there for perhaps four hours, but it has only just hit her, that smell. For the first hour or two she did nothing but survey the blue skeins on her hands, scrutinising the rocky spurs of her knuckles and trying to stretch the fingers long since frozen by arthritis. All that time on her hands and hardly a thought for the girl. Just the skin on her hands and the colours beneath. Then unshaped thoughts whizzed by like fireworks. She can't recall what any of the thoughts were, they sped by so quickly. And now the smell. Oh, what she would do for a toffee, something to sweeten the anxiety.

The nurse comes by again with a copy of *People's Friend*. Something to read while you're waiting, she says.

Jenny sets the magazine on her lap. Perhaps later she will be able to stomach the pictures, but not now. She feels a stab of resentment at the nurse for bringing it to her.

Can I fetch you a cup of tea? says the nurse.

Somewhere beyond the double doors lies the girl. They say she's in an iron lung but this means more or less nothing to her mother who finds it hard enough to imagine a real one. The link from cause to effect is bewildering. One moment the girl is out playing on her bicycle, the next she is lying on the pavement with some stranger cradling her head, her breath as raspy as steam from a boiler and a trickle of red leaving her mouth. And now there's the iron lung. Everything between is confusion. Jenny sees herself kneeling on the pavement with her heart thumping against her ribs and a strange buzzing behind her eyes. A man is beside her with his hand on her arm, she is leaning over the body and parting the fine chestnut hair and then suddenly it hits her with a great force. This face isn't Rosie's face, this hair not Rosie's hair, and for a moment she feels herself slump. Her love for Rosie is a river without bridges. Something she cannot cross. Oh God Almighty, she thinks, what am I doing?

And now she waits for news of her daughter from the nurse in the brown uniform. Is she . . . ? The words shudder to a halt. The nurse leans towards her and rests a hand on her arm.

We'll have to wait for the doctor. I'd better get on.

And so Jenny waits. It is, after all, what she is good at. At the end of the waiting, the doctor appears from behind a double door, his buffed brown brogues clipping across the lino.

Mrs Page? He speaks in the voice of someone whose time is of immeasurable importance. Your daughter has a collapsed lung. And pleurisy.

Pleurisy. She feels relief bubble up. Pleurisy isn't so bad. Half the East End has pleurisy.

The doctor stares down at her through his glasses. How long has she been in this condition? he asks.

It only just come on her.

Mrs Page, he says, slowing down now, making much of each word. Your daughter must have been ill for some time.

The edge in his voice gives him away. He's telling her she's a liar and a bad mother. Her daughter is ill and a man from Up West with a fancy life and a nice dry house, a man who travels to work on a train and eats in restaurants, is telling her she doesn't look out for her own daughter. She wants to scream. She bites her throbbing lip. Tears muster in her eyes.

Mrs Page, the doctor sighs, speaking quickly again now, I think your daughter has tuberculosis, and I think it is likely that she has had tuberculosis for some time. I'm afraid we're going to have to put her on the danger list.

He knows, she thinks, he knows about her life, about little William and Rosie and the fact that they grew up with cardboard for shoes and went hungry when there was no work. He knows it all and in some obscure way he thinks it's all her fault. The result, somehow, of her choices. He has no idea how few choices there have been.

You know what tuberculosis is? the doctor is saying.

She shrugs and looks at her shoes.

They called tuberculosis the White Death. In the late 1940s there was still no cure for it in Britain. The most that could be done for the patient was to extend the period of their life with rest. 'Lungers' were stabilised in hospital then shipped off to sanatoria where their illness might be ameliorated and the likelihood of their infecting others reduced. In the 1920s the average stay in sanatoria was four or five months. Those discharged in the first stages of the disease had one sixth of the life expectancy of a healthy person, those discharged in the second stage were one twentieth as likely to live a full life. Even after the second war, one fifth of TB sufferers died.

The sanatoria were crowded, lonely places. As if to emphasise their contagion, patients had their own sheets, cutlery, bowls and spitting cups which were boiled and burned once the patient had died or temporarily recovered. The routine was as harsh as prison. Bells regulated every minute of the day. Patients were lined up on wheeled beds in elongated wards, forbidden for much of each day to move, read, wash or talk. In one typical sanatorium they were woken at seven and required to take their own rectal temperature. Those who were well enough took a hydrotherapy bath, after which the library opened for half an hour. The book selection was poor. Books on tuberculosis were not allowed. The period after bathing was for rest, with no talking. Lunch was usually some bland milk-based concoction and any patient who was too ill or too demoralised to eat would more or less be force fed. For those who were well enough, afternoon brought the 'grades', work of varying arduousness, from weaving to rock-breaking. Grades were followed by another rest break or 'rounds' for those who were well enough to walk in circles for an hour. Supper was brief, then, at ten o'clock, it was lights out.

Once a week all the beds were wheeled out while a char fumigated the walls and swept the floors and then the smell of cheap disinfectant would hang over the beds like a billboard, reminding each consumptive of his unclean state. Lungers had few visitors. The sanatoria rules forbade the sick from touching one another or even from talking much. For month after month they lay, lost and solitary, in long, sorrowful lines, many of them waiting to die.

The most common treatment was known as collapse. It provided some respite, though not a cure. The patients called the treatment gassing and dreaded it. The night before each gassing, a nurse would come by to administer morphine and calomel, then first thing in the morning there would be a shot of local anaesthetic and the patient would be curtained off from others on the same ward. At some point mid-morning a white-coated doctor would disappear behind the curtains and there would follow a terrible moaning as the thick gassing needle passed between the lunger's ribs and pricked the pleural membrane and the air began to billow in. By the afternoon, when the anaesthetic started to wear off, the patient would be delirious with pain and in four or five days, just as the pain had begun to ease, the gassing would begin again. It usually took three or four refills for the air to settle between the pleura. After this initial sequence the gassings would become less frequent; once every six weeks or so for the following three or four years, alternating with subcutaneous iron injections to compensate for the great loss of blood from coughing, and with sulphonamide injections to help contain the secondary infections.

If the gassing failed to stem the degeneration of a patient's lungs, the next procedure was to collapse the lungs some other way, either by crushing the consumptive's phrenic nerve in order to paralyse the diaphragm or by blowing up the abdomen like a balloon to force the diaphragm upwards into the thorax or, as a last, desperate measure, by removing the overlying ribs.

In lieu of any cure, the sanatoria doctors tried every kind of palliative. Patients were wheeled on to balconies and left in the frost and snow to 'breath the air'. The more modern sanatoria bombarded x-rays at the patients' failing lungs until their hair fell out. Radiation sickness often finished the job TB started, reducing its subjects to the thinnest wisp of life. Other, less well-equipped sanatoria favoured inhalations where patients were placed over fuming bowls of iodides, dyes, copper cyanurate, guaiacol, pig-spleen, silica, colloidal silver, copper, aluminium and antimony, lime and gypsum.

For now, the girl is transferred to an isolation unit in a long corridor painted cucumber green and filled, as might be expected, with the ugly sounds and dank smells of illness. The room itself is curtained-off. On the second day of her illness, her mother is allowed to visit.

Be prepared for a sight, the nurse says, opening the curtain.

The girl lies on a metal bed covered with a starched sheet, surrounded by the architecture of artificial life. Clamps invade her mouth, her throat, her arms. There are tubes and pipes in every orifice. It looks as though a metallic city has grown over her. The nurse rests a hand on Jenny's shoulder. Poor little thing, she says.

Will she . . . ? asks Jenny.

We don't know.

Back home in Altmore Avenue, visitors arrive for the evening – Dora, Emily Page, Frances Maud and a couple of cousins. Time blurs by. Someone, Dora she thinks, puts the boy to bed and helps her into her night things. Her sleep is invaded by jarring dreams featuring Frenchie and Sarah and dear Rosie. For the second time in her life she feels she is drifting away.

The hospital says the girl has stabilised overnight.

Will she . . . ?

We can't say.

That day a lamb belly bearing a New Zealand stamp turns up at the café via the Goods Shed. It has to be cut and trimmed then stewed and the fat skimmed off and kept for frying slice. And quickly, before the coppers come calling. Then there are potatoes to peel and chips to cut and all the rest. Jenny goes home on her own that evening, exhausted and smelling of onions and animal fat. By eight the boy is in bed and she is alone. Half an hour later, Mrs MacReady walks in bringing sympathy and a rock bun.

Thought it might cheer the girl up an' all, poor little mite. 'Ere, Mrs P, I wouldn't mind a cup of tea. What is it then she's got, your little one?

Well . . . Jenny hesitates. The word tuberculosis rings too much of filth and poverty. The girl's got tubes in, she says. Her chilblains begin to throb.

Oh, I didn't know there was tubes.

No.

They sit in silence for a moment.

Listen, Mrs P, seeing there's tubes, what d'you say we cut the rock bun in two and each 'ave arf? says Mrs MacReady.

For weeks the girl seems to be walking a tightrope between life and death. The uncertainty eats at her mother's heart. On bad days everything frightens and constricts her: the bus to work, the slabs of liver she has to prepare in the café, the mound of potatoes awaiting peeling, the café customers, the airless streets of Silvertown. At other times, feeling seems to have left altogether. She inhabits nothingness. Her only sure thing is work.

Len spends most of his time avoiding her. This is probably a good thing, since they are in complete disagreement over their daughter's condition. Simply put, Len doesn't believe it. One moment, he says, she was well (he didn't ever check as such, but she certainly looked all right) and the next they are told she is gravely ill. Either the doctors are wrong or the girl is making it up. He wonders out loud if she has decided to be ill just to spite him, or perhaps to make him change his mind and let her stay on at school. A scammer only sees a scam.

The weeks trundle by and the girl's condition gradually improves. She is taken off the iron lung and is sent to a sanatorium and the answer to the question 'will she?' becomes 'yes, probably she will, but it'll take a long while'.

Long while my arse, says Len to this prognosis. She's needed in the caff.

Jenny's own return to the world happens rather sooner, during a morning in December. She is up early as usual when there is a light knock on the door and Terry Barger, the milkman, appears, wanting his weekly payment.

Nice morning it'll be, Mrs P, says Barger, tasting the air. He is always cheerful, this red-faced, mop-haired little man, and this in spite of a heart condition and having been in a Japanese POW camp and having no fingernails.

If you say so, Mr Barger, can't say as I see it meself, says Jenny. She takes in the milk, goes to the jar on the mantel and makes up a couple of shillings from odd coppers.

How's the nipper, Mrs P? He takes the money, lingers on the step for a moment, then reaching out a nailless hand, squeezes her arm. See you next week then Mrs P.

Jenny picks up twelve pounds of lamb liver from Paterson's and makes her way to the bus stop on the High Street, listening to the sound of traffic. In Silvertown, she stops off at the post office and is let in by the postmistress, Sally Springer, still dressed in her housecoat.

Come in, Mrs P, you know where the telephone is. I was just brewing a cuppa. Why don't you stop for one with us?

The sanatorium says the girl is no better but no worse either. Letting herself into the Cosy, Jenny hauls the liver over the counter and begins the task of scrubbing the floor and for a long, satisfying stretch of time, she loses herself in the job and is suddenly startled by the sound of the door opening and the bell clanging. Expecting a customer she rises and wipes her hands on the greasy fabric of her apron.

There, standing in the entrance to the café, wearing a blue calico dress and with her hair swept up in pins, is June. The honey blonde. For a moment the two of them stand fixed to their spots, embarrassed. Then June says, Well, here I am. I expect there's lots to be done. She begins taking off her jacket. A powerful sense of her fills the room. She pulls out an apron from her bag and ties the straps around her waist. Only with the girl away, and all, Len says he needs another pair of hands, she says, so . . . she manufactures a broad smile that shows off her brilliant little teeth . . . here I am.

And so there she was and there was nothing in this world Jenny could do about it.

That night Jenny makes her way down Altmore Avenue alone. At number 5 she notes the newly whitened steps. Number 11's milk still stands outside the door. Tips, the Tiptons' black and white cat, plugs their doorway. Number 17 is having a row. She avoids Mrs MacReady sweeping her step by crossing to the other side and pretending to post a letter. Her head drums and her heart is very frail. Because now she understands. She understands Len's absences, his mood swings and his overheated temper. She understands his impatience, his new clothes, his motor car. She understands the moment on the way back from Southend when June's hand slid to Len's knee. It could have been a bump in the road. But it wasn't. Now she knows what it really was. Exactly what it really was.

CHAPTER 18

All through the autumn of 1947 the river batters the jetties and quays and by mid-winter it has spewed brown water on to the streets, breaching piled sandbags and creeping into the stairwells of the tenement buildings and through the hallways of the terraces of Silvertown, where it freezes and trips up old women only just accustomed to the snares and potholes left by the war. A terrible cold snap follows. But when it leaves, something of Silvertown's malaise goes with it.

Come the spring of 1948, men begin to nail down new jetties all along the frontage, from Bugsby's Reach to Gallions Point. Long abandoned quays are repaired and the river slime cleared from them. Where the old wharves have been blasted away, new and larger wharves are hastily constructed with Finnish timber from the Surrey Quays and with concrete milled at Siley's in North Woolwich. On a weekday at high tide, the river once more runs black with tugs and lighters, bringing cargoes that bulge from the transit sheds and keep the dock trains busy. Lorries are strung out along every approach road. On Friday mornings, the queues stretch all the way to Canning Town in the west and as far as the gasometers at Beckton on the eastern side. On Friday evenings too, after the whistles sound, a tide of men and women pour from the factories and the dock gates with their pay packets, dropping off at the clubs and pubs along their route home or else catching ferries or walking through the river tunnel to their rooms and tenements in South Woolwich. There are lines outside the fish and chip shops. Beggars appear, and on dry nights the pavements are patterned with chalk scenes of London done by men who have seen too much in the war to settle to any other way of living.

Business continues to blossom at The Cosy Corner Café. The harsh winter and floods bring in customers. So do the booming factories and docks. And so does June. June bubbles with ideas. The baby-blue paint is unsuitable. Can't they repaint in brown? The lino is scuffed and too tattered. She's heard of some new stuff that keeps its shine. Today, what June reckons they need is a frigidaire. When Len comes in she'll tell him.

Lenny, she says, waiting till he is sitting in the kitchen with a cup of strong tea in his hand and a Senior wedged between his lips, I'm thinking maybe we should modernise.

Len looks up from the table a moment and glances at his wife peeling potatoes in the sink.

A frigidaire is what I'm thinking, Lenny. Like what they have in America.

Len takes a long drag of his cigarette and begins absentmindedly to stroke the inside of his palm with the yellowed fingers of his other hand.

Keep ahead of the competition, Lenny, is all I'm thinking.

No harm in that. A frigidaire. He rolls the word around his mouth. Well, I ain't saying yes but I ain't saying no.

When June is around Len is like a cartoon dog, with a panting tongue and a thumping tail and a sit-up-and-beg attitude. June can play him like a tuppenny whistle. And although some may — and do — call June common, she is in fact that rare thing in the East End — a woman who can see her way up and out of the Abyss, a little knot of ambition in the long haul to the top.

Len checks to see that his wife isn't watching, then pinches June on the arse and winks.

We'll see, he says.

She uses the same technique on the customers. One lunchtime, just after she begins work at the café, Red and Hanny storm in with dark-looking faces, in search of Joey Flanagan, the union man, who is at that moment sitting at the back of the café giving his order to June. One of the men in Hanny's gang has taken a hit from a swinging crane on a discharge job. The man bowled over into the hatch and got himself crushed under a pile of dislodged sacks. The sacks were full of walnuts. So it was said, the hatchman, Sam Riley, hadn't been keeping his eye on the sacks and had let the discharge get uneven. He'd cleared off before the heat could get to him. Red and Hanny have just returned from breaking the news to the man's wife and now they are looking for Sam, who happens to be a cousin of Joey Flanagan's.

Flanagan, says Hanny, swinging into the seat next to the man. I'll be straight with you. We want Sam Riley. We ain't gonna do nothin' to the boy 'cept walk him to the widow's house and get him to account for hisself, but we want him, Joey, a man needs to make things right.

Flanagan's face glows then he just shrugs and says, It's a safety issue, innit. We got the union on to it.

Now Flan, says Hanny, I appreciate that, you know I do, but there's business to sort out here.

Like I already said, Hanny, it's union business, says Flanagan, giving an impression of finality and returning to his order. June, you got any of that bread pudding left?

Hanny and Red eye each other.

Flanagan, sighs Hanny, with menace in his voice, I'm sorry it's got ter this but we ain't leaving till you tell us where Sammy Riley is at.

Bread pudding it is, says June, tapping her pad. What about you gents?

Flanagan knows what we're after, says Red.

Well that's as might be, but I don't. June scribbles something on her notepad. She flashes a wink at Hanny. Oo, Hanny, she says, that scowl don't arf suit yer. You should do it more often.

For an instant Hanny sits immobilised, then the scowl melts like a cheap ice cream. The men exchange awkward glances. Finally Flanagan pipes up, When are you next on the menu, June?

Ha ha soldier, remember your manners!

I don't remember nothing 'fore I met you, Juney. Flanagan takes the Capstan from his lips, pinches it out and sticks the doofer behind his ear. What about you fellas?

Nothing, says Hanny.

Zero, says Red.

From behind the hatch in the kitchen, Jenny watches with envy. Oh, you've got to give it to her. On the surface she's all giggle and wobble, but underneath she's as tough as boiled brisket. And that's how it is with June. When Hanny and Red come in next they will be all Morning, Mrs P, where's June? June in today, Mrs P? When you expecting that June?

Before July and after May, Jenny will say.

Oh right-o, Mrs P, they'll reply, but they won't laugh. Not a bit of it.

During those first weeks, a frigidaire appears, the lino is fixed, the clientele expands, but the reason for June's employment in the café is almost forgotten. For month after month the girl lies immobile. Then slowly she begins to sit up. By the summer following her admission to the sanatorium she is well enough to rise from her bed and shuffle around the ward on unsteady feet. In the afternoons she reads books but the doctors say it will be a long time before she is ready to come home. Jenny's visits are painful affairs. What to say to the girl? Always reading, reading.

Mum, you bring anything to read? the girl will say.

Here, have this bit of Turkish Delight.

I don't want Turkish Delight.

You can read what's on the packet, Jenny will say.

Next time, Mum, bring me a book about animals.

Len has his own theories. If she's well enough to bury her head in them bleedn books, she's well enough to put in a bit of time in the caff, where she's needed. I got malaria in the bleedn jungle and I'm still here. We should have her down the caff chopping veg, that'll keep her busy. She'll be right as rain in no time.

Jenny wants to call the sanatorium from the telephone at the post office.

Len, she says, I need a bit of cash for the telephone.

Oh, he says, as though this is of no consequence to him. He digs in his pocket and pulls out a few coins.

Get us a packet of Seniors while you're out, he says. And don't be long.

The post office is nearly empty. Behind the counter sit the Springers, Pete and Sally.

'Noon, says Pete Springer. Just help yerself, pet.

For two and a half years Jenny has been ringing first the hospital, then the sanatorium from the telephone in the Springers' back room, only to be told the same thing, that the girl is stable but her recovery will take some time. And then, one day in the spring of 1948, Jenny puts down the phone in the Springers' back room and walks out into the post office with a smile on her face.

Good news, Mrs P? says Pete Springer.

They're saying she can come out tomorrer, for a bit.

Oh that's grand, that is.

Yes. It is grand, she says. Not wanting to return to the café she wanders to the swing bridge overlooking the Vic Dock. The air has grown steadily warmer and the sky more clear. She can just make out the gasometers at Beckton, risen to their full height today like a row of iron lungs. From now on, she thinks, her life will be like breathing out. The girl will return to work in the caff and June will leave and the whole dirty business will disappear as fast as a sigh.

She travels to Wanstead on the bus and picks the girl up in the hallway of the sanatorium.

I got you something nice for tea, she says.

The girl does her best to look pleased.

They sit in the kitchen at Altmore Avenue in silence, not knowing what to say.

Well I dunno, says Len finally, sucking in his cigarette and gargling the slime from his lungs. The girl looks all right to me. Can she peel 'taters?

Ask 'er, says Jenny.

Well, can yer? says Len.

S'pose, says the girl, caught between defiance and pride.

The following day she is peeling for England and coughing all over the sandwiches.

She don't talk much, says Len at the day's end, but she ain't half a little grafter.

There is no question now of the girl staying on at school and taking up teacher training. She settles back into Altmore Avenue and goes to work at The Cosy Corner Café and for a while nothing more is said about the matter. The battle between father and daughter dims, the victory temporarily snatched from both of them by tuberculosis.

A few weeks later, Jenny and the girl are travelling on the bus together with ten pounds of liver. The sun is out but with it comes the first chill of autumn. The bus grinds to a halt at a traffic light on the Barking Road. Up ahead there are roadworks, and a diversion sign directing traffic off to the right.

You know, Jenny says, once you're up and running, pet, it'll just be us. She pats her daughter's fragile hand, wondering if the girl has guessed at the truth. Just us, she says.

The girl returns to her book without giving a response. Every day she sits with her mother on the bus. She does her work and eats her tea and even joins in conversations from time to time, but only her body actually lives in Altmore Avenue. The rest of her inhabits a different world altogether.

The bus swings along a spur road then down into a grid of residential streets. They scrape past trees then turn left again along the diversion. At the top of this road, the girl's attention is caught by something going on in the street below. She puts down her book and peers out.

What you lookin' at? says Jenny.

Dad, says the girl. He's got June with him. She presses her nose against the window pane.

Let me see.

Below them, behind the wheel of a brand new motor, is the figure of Len Page, and, next to him, adjusting the collar of a beautiful beaver coat, is June. Jenny heaves the bag of liver closer and adjusts her hair.

Like I said, once you're up and running, then we'll see.

The following week a cargo of mouldy tobacco is burned at the King's Pipe on the KGV. For two days Silvertown is lost in a smoke sea. Men and women cover their faces in handkerchiefs and snatches of cloth. It is all too much for the girl. By the end of the second day her breath is stuttering and she begins coughing blood. Leave her a while, see how she gets on, Len says.

Two days after that they have no choice but to take her back to hospital.

You should have brought her in before now, tuts the doctor disapprovingly.

Listen, Sonny Boy, says Len, landing the doctor a heavy pat on the shoulder. You should have got her better.

Jenny Page watches her daughter go. Hers is a different story, to be told another time. The point is that the girl's return has made no difference. June has lodged herself inside the family like a stain that no soap or scrubbing brush will shift.

CHAPTER 19

One evening in the spring of 1950, Jenny is sitting at a table in West Ham dog track finishing up a plate of ham and eggs. She has grown thinner since the war. Arthritis has begun to creep into her legs and hips and her eyes are watery from the years at the treadle. The bountiful hair is now stippled with grey. To say she looks her age – forty-seven – isn't really helpful. She looks the age people look when they are nearly, but not quite, done in.

Opposite Jenny, at the same table, sits June, dressed in a plain blue frock with a modern-looking string of shell beads and with her hair pinned back at the sides and curled at the bottom. She is younger than Jenny by ten years or so, but to say she looks her age isn't really helpful either. She looks the age people look when the world has just dropped into their lap.

On the other side of the table sit Len and Harry and a man in a flat tweed cap. They are listening to Len describe his newest motor, bought recently from an American military man who was on his way back home. A fancy motor it is too. A Caddy, Jenny thinks. Something like a Caddy. The man in the flat cap seems impressed. Poor Harry is tipsy as always, harmless as always, and staring into space, imagining himself anywhere but here.

The crowd gathered at Prince Regent Lane for the Tuesday dog meet is large and enthusiastic, though not quite as large and not quite so enthusiastic as it was before the war. There are reasons for this. The population of West Ham, once 35,000, is now less than half that number. Some of this can be accounted for by the loss of life in the war, some of it is as a result of the decline in manufacture and heavy industry in the area, but mostly it is because there is so little housing left standing in the borough. Some residents have been moved to temporary cities of prefabs, luxurious by pre-war standards, with hot and cold running water and indoor toilets, and the remainder have taken up the council's offer of a house or a flat on one of the vast new council estates on what were once the boggy fields of Essex. These estate dwellers may have been separated from their families and friends, they may not know their butcher or the man who delivers their milk, they may well find themselves commuting through the patchy countryside on greenline buses to work, but their houses and flats are clean, well-insulated and free of bugs and damp. They have a bathroom and hot water and the satisfaction of knowing that when an opportunity came their way they took it.

Len Page's ambition is altogether sharper. There's the café and the Caddy and between times there are the dogs. For nearly two years now, he has been a dog owner. At the last count he had about forty. They live in a row of crude brick hutches at kennels in Plaistow. Len visits them often. He loves their breathy, swishing bodies and their unquestioning submission. Of the forty, he has two particular favourites, Silvertown Streak and Silvertown Sailor. Sailor is perhaps the more beautiful of the two, an elegant buff with liquorice eyes and a white bib, but Streak is the character, burly, swaggering, all unburdened energy and enthusiasm. Whenever Len visits the kennels, Streak is the first dog he heads for. He rumples his coat, laughs and whispers sweet nothings in his leather ears.

The Edge, he says. You can tell when a pup has the Edge. There's an Edgeness about him you can feel. Now, Streak boy here, he has the Edge.

Once a week Len shows his face at Prince Regent Lane, enough to be noticed but not so often that it looks as though he has nowhere else to go. Usually he is in the company of a 'known face'. He and the known face will sit at the same spot in the bar and nod towards other dogmen and exchange snippets of dogman politics. He can tell you who had a punch-up with whom, over what, and in which pub. If a dog has had a laxative put in its food, or glass powder rubbed into its pads, then Len will know about it. He can summon up the form record of almost any dog you care to name, and many a dock copper or PLA official relies on him for tips. He is on first-name terms with all the bookies in the betting enclosure and keeps them sweet with drinks and free meals at The Cosy Corner Café. The staff at Prince Regent Lane call him guvnor.

On this particular night, Len is quietly tipping Silvertown Streak. For the last few weeks Streak has been on terrible form. But tonight something – call it instinct – tells Len Page that Streak is going to run like the clappers.

The East End is a conman's cornucopia. The docks, in particular, are so ripe with opportunity you'd have to be mad or a saint not to take advantage. Scamming is a weapon of the weak, a small subversion of a system that prices most cargo out of the range of the men who load and unload it and leaves them and their families constantly vulnerable to sapping poverty and the local loanshark. At the time of Len's ascendance, the whole East End is a complex web of scams with the docks at its heart. New terms have to be invented for the art of the fiddle. Take an 'oversider'. If a ship is oversiding or working on the buoys, then like as not, some of the cargo won't make it into the midstream barge. The donkey man who operates the winch will be in on the scam and he'll skew the winch every so often so that some of the cargo lands in the water, to be attached to a marker, or left to float, and picked up at low tide by mudlarks. Then there's the 'sworn weight' scam, where the men sworn in to weigh goods will suddenly forget how to read the scales. In the 'salvage' scam, the salvage workers do a little private salvaging on the side. In the 'stackman' scam, the stackmen fill a lorry just a little too full and the lorry man makes sure some of the extra load drops off the back of the vehicle. For the petty pilferer, the docks are an open sesame. At low level it is easy enough to avoid detection. Dockers twist stockings into dolly bags, fill them with pilfered tea and hang them inside their trouser legs. Bottles of whisky and rum and joints of meat disappear this way, too. Surplus pilfered goods go into 'lock-ups' or 'goods sheds' for a couple of days before being offered cut rate in the pubs.

In the way of the most successful players, Len keeps his scams to himself. It is never quite clear what he has got himself into. Most likely he dabbles in dog doping and fixing bets, smuggling, fencing, a bit of black marketeering here and there. He has friends who look out for him and others whom he pays to turn a blind eye. Every so often the coppers pay a visit to Altmore Avenue then go away again. Most likely he is paying them, too. Jenny thinks with bitter irony that the only people not in Len's pocket are his wife and children. He doesn't believe in giving them wages. They are only family, after all.

It's easier to guess how Len spends his money than how he makes it. There's the motor, and June's beaver coat and jewellery. He has a new set of clothes, all bespoke, and a gold-plated watch. But old habits persist. His wife still has to squeeze the housekeeping money from him and the rest of his family live in poverty. If anything, their little home in Altmore Avenue is more dismal than it ever was. The cold westerlies rush through the kitchen window where the frame has shrunk, the damp has clambered under the windowsills and flowered into mildew. Outside in the yard, Len's dogs have demolished the cabbage plot and the chrysanthemum bed. The Andy shelter is now filled with crates of beeswax polish and Knight's Castille soap, Tate and Lyle's sugar cubes and tubs of Brylcreme. There are no longer any chickens in the privy but the door is hanging off and the floor is caked in mould. Always fond of birds, Len has taken to keeping canaries and racing pigeons but he's not home often enough to look after them. Every month or so there are mass deaths but Len doesn't care. The breeder gives him wholesale price.

Len's ambition is understandable, admirable even, but also unforgivable, not because it falls outside the law but because it falls outside the realms of human decency. By now it is a runaway train, careering along tracks built by hearts weaker than his own. The way the East End works, Len can't simply rely on talent, drive or opportunity. He is forced to depend on a troupe of cronies, his little circle of pushovers and bent coppers and acolytes and, yes, family – a whole crew of, as he sees it, second-raters and half-wits who'll dig their graves for him then smile when he doesn't return the favour. They are a dead weight he cannot shirk off. He hates needing them this much.

Tonight, though, he needs none of them. Tonight all he needs is luck and Silvertown Streak. There are five minutes to go before the tenth race and Streak is at the long odds of 15 to 1. Two or three men, including the wiry copper, stand to make a fat wad from Streak tonight and Len is in for fifty per cent. The handlers lead the runners out into the arena. The number one, a large black dog called Daddy's Boy, is followed by Streak. At three is a brindle bitch known as Solomon's Seal followed by an ageing ex-open dog, Xanadu, at four, Missy Grey at five and some outside shot no one recognises in the wide six.

Blow me, says the wiry copper sitting next to Harry, if your pup ain't got his blood up.

The thing is, says Len, winking, you never can tell with a dog.

That's it on the nail, guvnor, says the copper, smiling. You never can.

They wait for the dogs to be placed in their traps then move over to the balcony to get a better look. The crowd stills, the hare runs, the traps open and the dogs are suddenly flinging themselves across the dirt track. They shear around the first bend, the number one in the lead. On the back straight, Streak inches closer, overtaking the one dog on the scramble for the rail at the second bend. As they round the corner, Streak is gunning, his jaws leaking bloody foam and he's ahead by a length now and looking invincible. When they reach the finishing mast you can hear the collective gasp from the crowd and see the shock in their faces that this 15 to 1 has-been, this no-mark, has just wiped out all the competition.

Well I never, says Len, slapping the copper on the back, shaking his head in mock wonder and lifting his eyes around the room to see who's looking. It's my round.

They make their way to the bar. Len Page waves at those he knows, exchanges a few words with whose who count, then strolls to the back bar where a group of PLA plods he recognises are drinking Trubrown.

Gents, Len says, opening up his pack of Senior Service and handing it round. You on splits tonight? He runs an eye over the men's suits. Or off-duty?

We're off.

Thought I'd buy you fellas a pint to celebrate, like. Len takes his wad from his pocket and begins counting notes.

That's big of you, Lenny.

When you've finished, come and say hello to the . . . He hesitates for an instant. To the wife.

Which one? pipes up one wit.

The men laugh and wink.

Whichever one you like, says Len. Whichever you like.

At the front of the bar, Harry is fetching drinks for Jenny and June.

Know what, Harry? says June suddenly, her eyes trained on the back of the bar. I fancy some of them whelks from that stall we passed. You wouldn't be a lovely chap, would you? Would you?

She giggles, lifts her drink to her pretty mouth and drains the glass.

And get us another drink, darling? Oh go on.

The two women sit awkwardly for a moment before the man in the flat cap launches into an analysis of Streak's unexpected brilliance in the tenth.

Oh Harry, June says when the whelks arrive, they don't half look tough. It's not me I'm thinking about so much as Jen, with her teeth and all. She throws her head jauntily to one side. You wouldn't take them back, pet, get us some cockles instead?

He would of course. Of course he would.

There. June plumps her hair. I don't know, she sighs. Everything feels different tonight.

Just then Len bounces over and, smiling, says, Come on, June, I'll take you and Harry down the kennels. See Streak before they take him back to Plaistow. He looks about. Oh, Harry ain't here. Well, just you and me then.

Oh I don't know. June pulls back her chair. I look a mess.

You look . . . Len stands over her for a moment, staring at her face, its familiar contours and lines, the face of the woman he should have married. You look a picture.

In miserable silence Jenny and the copper watch the pair go off.

Who's gonna tell Harry? asks the copper, as Harry appears through the crowd holding a mug of cockles in his hand. Jenny shakes her head. There's no need to tell Harry because Harry decided long ago that he didn't want to know.

It is very late when Len and June return, laughing, their eyes filled with the reflections of time well wasted. The bar has closed and the remaining customers have decamped to the dogmen's room at the back, where a game of gin rummy has begun.

June, let's go home, says Harry, grabbing for his wife's arm.

Sliding away from his grasp, June lights a cigarette and blows the smoke from her nostrils.

Shut up, Harry.

C'mon Sonny Boy, says Len, taking his friend by the elbow. Don't be a creeping Jesus. Let's spin them winnings on a game of cards.

I don't want a game of cards, says Harry, sounding sober now. I want to go home with my wife.

Len and June exchange anxious glances.

Listen Sonny Boy, says Len, patting his friend on the back. The thing is, your wife don't want to go home jess yet. Do yer, June?

No, says June. No, I want to watch the gin rummy.

So how's about it, Harry?

Harry blinks his bloodshot eyes and sighs. All right, Lenny. All right.

Some way through the second game, a conversation starts up on the subject of the docks. The heavyweight to the right of Len who has been steadily losing money reckons the docks are doomed. I give 'em five years, he mutters.

The man to the right of him checks his cards and strokes his ginger moustache. You don't know what you're talking about, mate, with respect. You seen how much traffic comes into them docks on the high tide? Can't move for ships.

Oh it looks all right now, I'll grant yer, says the heavyweight, but you mark, they'll be laying off men soon enough.

Blimey, says the ginger 'tash, laying down his cards. We got ourselfs a right Laughing Boy here and he just got beat at rummy an' all.

Later, after the policemen have left and the last of the players and their wives are fastening up their coats and going out into the night, Jenny finds herself in the ladies' powder room thinking about the heavyweight's words when June steps in and, taking a comb from her handbag, begins teasing her hair.

Oh there you are, Jenny. Didn't know where you'd got to. To cover the lie, she turns on the tap and wets her comb. Lovely dog, that Streak. Lenny likes his runners with a bit of spirit in 'em. I've noticed that.

Jenny shuts her eyes. She wants to say, Have him, you've got him anyway.

Do you want to know what I think? I don't think Lenny ever really settled here. June returns the comb to her bag and brings out her compact. He's a country fella. She begins powdering her nose. Wouldn't you say, Jenny? I mean, you know him better than anyone else. Isn't that what you'd say? Well, isn't it?

June continues dabbing powder on her skin, softly at first, then with an odd, almost wild vigour.

Well, I'm surprised you don't agree, Jenny, I really am. 'Cause only the other day Len says to me, June, what do you think to a café in the country? And I says, well, you'll have to talk it over with your wife, but he says, Oh it's only a little idea I've been having and no more than that. There, do you think this hair suits me? Without waiting for a reply, she begins plumping her fringe. So anyway, I says to him, Lenny, I really don't know what Jenny will think of this because, you know, she's a Londoner. A real

Londoner. She don't like the country. June reaches into her bag once more, pulls out her lipstick and begins swirling it madly around her mouth.

That's right, ain't it, Jenny? You're a Londoner, ain't yer? A real Londoner.

Jenny Page stares at the image of the woman beside her.

Well that's better, says June. She picks up her handbag and swings out of the ladies', the beaver coat swirling behind her like a dark tornado.

CHAPTER 20

Jenny is at the sink, skinning a pair of sheep's kidneys and picking off the clinging remnants of grey fat. Len is standing by the counter with a sharp knife and a dozen pounds of pig liver. It is June's morning off. Jenny looks forward to these mornings with only Len in the kitchen, not so much because she enjoys his company but because she can persuade herself that things are as they once were. Outside there is warm, syrupy sunshine. It's the kind of day that usually signals slack business in the café and a chance to catch up on the week's chores before the rain sets in again, driving the men indoors for hot faggots and sweet tea. Turning back from the sink, Jenny's eye falls on the figure of Bill Walter, sitting in his usual corner, his jaw flapping open like the lid of a coal scuttle, method-ically working some piece of gristle between upper and lower jaws. Solid, predictable Bill. In a while he'll pop his head round the door and say, Ho there, Jenny, lovely day. Sweet, predictable Bill.

The front door opens, shaking the bell hung over it. Wiping his hands on his apron, Len goes to the counter but he's soon back, looking troubled and edgy. You can serve them lot. He returns to his liver. I'm too busy. Two bacon sarnies, tea.

She picks up the knife and a kidney and finishes skinning it, the urinal smell slipping back down into the plug hole. Then, taking two rashers from the grill pan, she wipes the knife on a slice of bread and presses the dough into the bacon, waiting for the grease to seep through. She calls out the order and from the front of the café a black man in a London Transport uniform appears.

Ain't seen you in 'ere before, she says.

I juss started de route, says the black man, smiling. Me shift end diss time here.

She finds herself staring at the white stripe of his teeth.

I din know you fellas ate bacon, she says.

The black man tips back his head and laughs.

Missus, that's de Muslims and dem Jews there you tinking of.

Oh, says Jenny. She returns to the kitchen, smiling to herself. Len is still hanging over his liver, teasing out the pipes and cutting through the gristle. A beetle, perhaps it is a cockroach, trickles across the lino towards the grill. Jenny runs her tongue across her teeth, checking for where the denture fix is wearing thin. The beetle, or whatever it is, creeps back along the lino in the direction it has just come. Cup of tea? she says, and not waiting for an answer puts the kettle on to boil. He waits for his tea in silence, takes a sip, then like a swollen sandbag, he bursts. Who thinks them nig-nogs can drive a London bus like a white man? This ain't Calcutta, this is England! His eyes are rolling about the room. When I think of Tommy, when I think of Ria and little Daisy . . . She watches his eyes spring tears. He starts at the liver again, chopping the maroon slabs into uneven chunks. I didn't stew in them swamps to have no jungle bunnies moving in next door, bringing their diseases with 'em, nicking our jobs. He is sweating now. Jenny swallows and gathers herself and hopes for the best. For a moment she wonders what is going on in her husband's mind or even in his heart, that busy back bar she has never entered, but then the kettle begins to stir and it's time to make a cup of tea.

By the afternoon, rain is falling on Silvertown and the café is beginning to get busy. Finishing his shepherd's pie and apple crumble and sweet tea, Bill Walter pops his head around the door into the kitchen and says, Ho there, Jenny, not such a lovely day today but seeing you's jess cheered me up, then he is out the front door, licking his chops. A group of strikers come in for a while before setting off to the pub. Len waits for June to arrive then disappears, claiming to have business elsewhere. Off to see his dogs, most likely. All afternoon the café fills and empties, and June bustles about, stabbing orders on the spike, plumping her hair in the mirror by the toilet. Cigarette smoke fills the café's blue interior. At six, half an hour before closing time, Jenny sets about washing the floor.

I'm off now, announces June, tying a scarf with a red rose print around her head. If it's all the same to you.

Jenny looks about the café at the unwashed tables, the scattered chairs not yet stacked on the table tops, the empty mugs and here and there the remains of someone's meal.

There's tables to be wiped down, June.

June glances at her watch. I'm late already, she snaps.

Jenny watches her walk towards the door. You think I'm a little mouse you can walk all over.

For a moment June stands there. Well, Jane Fulcher, that's exactly what you are.

The sound of her old name floods into a gap in Jenny's heart like drain water. She starts, steadying herself on the handle of her mop. Her hands are shaking. It is as though they have reached the root of everything and there will never be anything more to say. Then June turns back towards the door and disappears out into the street.

And so it goes on, this low-level warfare, from week to week, from month to month, and from year to creeping year.

*

One day in early September 1952, in the middle of a week of humid heat and drifting, squally rain, Len drives to the café early and on his own and hurries inside carrying a parcel.

Morning, he says.

Jenny looks up from wiping the tables. The years have treated him well. He is heavier than he once was, but still upright and elegant. His boiled hair is thinner but more distinguished now. As for Jenny, she no longer has any pretence to physical attractiveness. She has shrunk so much in recent years that she looks like a whippet. Her face has become beaky and her hands clubbed with arthritis. Her hair is thinning and age spots have begun creeping across her skin, from which blue veins bulge like road markings. For an instant, looking at him standing there, she remembers how much she once liked him, loved him even.

Morning, she says, a little nervously.

Unwrap it then, he says, holding out the parcel.

She unwraps the parcel gingerly, expecting she doesn't know what. She lays the paper to one side and parts the tissue to reveal a beige gabardine raincoat, looks at him in disbelief.

Get it out then, he says.

She shakes the coat free from the paper, then holds the fabric to her body. A beauty, three-quarters lined, with bone buttons, patch pockets and top stitching around the collar. A practical coat, a handsome coat, the gabardine finely woven, the stitching attentive and in a style that will not date. She has never seen such a gorgeous thing.

So what d'yer think? he says.

It's . . . it's . . . She loses the thread. Who is it for?

Who d'yer bleedn think?

She feels bewildered now. She wishes she had a lemon bon bon in her mouth.

June? she says.

Later on that evening, back home by herself in Altmore Avenue, she drapes the coat around her shoulders, anxious not to commit it to a proper fitting in case he changes his mind and takes it away. She admires herself in the hallway mirror, twirls round to see it move. The fabric swishes about, all twists and switchbacks. She runs her fingers down its seams. And the lining, too, some new, modern fabric. She swings her tiny self around again, smiling, and wonders how she might look if she had her own teeth, if she were sixteen again, with a few sweets jangling in her pocket. What can he be cooking up?

She doesn't have to wait long to find out. The thing is, he says at closing time the next day, when everyone else has left. The thing is, the East End ain't like it used to be.

No, she says.

Do you remember when we were courtin', how it was? We knew where we were, old girl. We didn't have much but we knew what was what.

She wants to ask what happened, but he has come to her and she is wearing his coat and she has learned to keep her mouth shut.

The thing is, this bleedn place is going to the dogs. They got coloureds driving buses. He shakes his head. If he were not so guarded she might have seen his wounded pride. So I've decided, he says, I've decided we're getting out the East End, old girl. We're goin' to the country.

She doesn't feel like going straight home that evening but there are few places a woman can go on her own. If only Dora hadn't left they might have walked together along the old childhood routes. She wanders down Silvertown Way towards Lyle Park, passing Johnny Donal standing on the corner of the road opposite Tate and Lyle's at Plaistow Wharf.

Evenin', Mrs P.

You not gone 'ome yet, Johnny?

I never go 'ome till I see the guvnor's left, Mrs P.

How long you gonna stand there, Johnny?

Till they give me back my job, Mrs P. That's all I want, my job back.

How long you been there now?

Two years, Mrs P, comin' up. That's a tidy coat you got on, Mrs P.

Come into the caff tomorrer and I'll fetch you a nice bit of shepherd's pie.

Johnny Donal lifts his cap and scrapes his hand along the unruly curls. I appreciate everythin' what you done for me, Mrs P. They gimme the heave-ho but I didn't do nothin' wrong, see.

She has heard this so many times now it is like listening to the pigeons cooing in the park.

A man's gotta stand up for hisself, says Johnny Donal, sounding forlorn. You understand that, dontcha, Mrs P?

As the sun begins to bend to the horizon, Jenny finds a spot on a bench in Lyle Park where she sits sucking lemon bon bons and brooding. I know we got our differences, Len had said, but some things a man does and some things he don't and a man don't quit his family. If she came it might be different, he had said. He couldn't promise anything, but maybe, he had hinted, his ways would shift with the change of air. Anything was possible, he'd said. Why was she finding it so hard to believe him?

Len's gift has always been to understand the rules; he knows which ones are brittle and will break under pressure, and which are supple and can be bent and woven and put to use. But Jenny has her talents, too. She knows how to patch holes, to repair and mend, but Len has the instinct for how the fabric itself is made.

Until that moment she has never fully understood how much he needs her, or someone like her. His family have been collateral in the progression of his ambition, his bond, the reason other men trust him. Without them, Len Page is just a country boy with a big mouth.

Jenny checks her watch and taps the glass. The lemon bon bon cracks on her tongue. She catches sight of the massive frame of Bill Walter in the watch glass, bulldozing his way towards her.

How you doin', pet? He crumples beside her, pulls a red rubber ball from his pocket and throws it for his dog. They sit in silence for a moment. Then, What brings you down this way?

Oh, she says, thinking.

He shakes his head and tuts in mock disapproval. Well that won't do.

The dog bounds back with the ball in its mouth, its tail wagging. Cheery fella.

Oh, says Bill. Me old dog there? Yes, always on top of the world. Retired runner. Speedy little bugger in his day, they say. Made a bob or two for his owner. I call 'im Bosun.

He signals Bosun to drop the ball then reaches out and gently pulls it from his mouth. The dog lurches in thrilled anticipation. Bill raises his arm and bowls the red ball across the grass and Bosun spins after it, into the far corner of the park next to the vast white tankers of the Shell-Mex petroleum store.

Olive don't like him tearing about the house. Thinks she's gonna trip over him. He picks up a stick and begins twirling it in his hand. Oh, he says, realising then how little she knows about him. Olive's me sister, like. You seen her in the caff a couple of times.

Jenny recalls a plump, dimply woman with purplish hair.

'Ere, says Bill, noticing the coat. What a get-up! You off to see the Queen?

In the furthest corner of the park the bushes begin moving, exposing from time to time the manic figure of Bosun, nose to the ground.

Don't be daft!

They smile and look in opposite directions.

It was a present from Len, she says, the raincoat.

Oh. Bill picks at the stick, then, retreating back to a safer subject, says, Poor Bosun nearly got the chop. Once they're a bit past it they knacker 'em, you know. He sucks on his tongue, the sound of his dentures filling the space between them. Don't seem right do it, really?

Well, says Jenny, the world ain't fair.

A gust of wind brings the thick spicy smell of molasses liquor from Tate's. Jenny loves that overpowering Silvertown smell, the sheer weight and history of sugar.

Len's selling the caff, moving out west to the country, she says finally. He's taking the boy . . . She feels her eyes filling. Bill reaches for her hand and rescues it from her lap. And he's taking June.

At that moment Bosun bounces back carrying a cow's hoof, a leftover from Knight's soapworks. Keeping hold of the dog's collar so he won't go bounding after it, Bill flings the hoof into the river, where it bobs up and begins its slow journey downstream towards the sea.

When I was a little boy, he says, I wanted to work on that river. Always down there I was, throwing pebbles, mudlarking on the foreshore.

The dog, confused, looks about for a moment then settles, panting, at his master's feet.

You going too, I s'pose?

He says he wants me to.

Ah then.

He pulls out a bag of aniseed pips, throws a couple to the dog and offers the bag to Jenny.

Only, begins Jenny. Only, I dunno if I will.

Oh? says Bill, sounding intrigued. His hands move to his face, scrubbing at the skin.

You never got to work on the river? she says, trying to change the subject.

Nah. There wasn't no work on the river. I went into the factories. But it wasn't no good. I'd be standing there, shifting boxes of marmalade, jess dreamin' about the river. Whenever the shift bell went I'd go straight down to the water. I'd sit and watch the river and I'd think. I jess liked to watch the boats and the gulls flying around. I'd throw in a few pebbles and wonder if it was the same over the other side as it was 'ere. I went downhill I did, and when the first war come I couldn't wait to get away. I hoped some Jerry'd shoot my bonce off so I wouldn't have to look at the river no more knowing I couldn't work on it. But I missed it. I couldn't stop thinking about it. I used to dream of that smell, you know, sugar and boiling bones and river mud. By the time the war ended, I couldn't wait to get back home. Didn't care what I did then, factories, lighters, whatever. But I ain't never wanted to go nowhere after that. The thing is, some places you're born to. They don't treat you as good as they oughta, but you're born to 'em and that's that.

A young couple are wandering beside the flowerbeds at the entrance to the park, the man in dockers' garb and the woman in a beige raincoat, bending to smell the roses spotted with factory smuts.

Best get back, Jenny says.

I'll walk yer to the bus stop, he says.

Ten minutes later she is standing beside the bus stop alone. The bus to Canning Town draws up, squeals to a halt and half a dozen men and women get off. She watches them disperse along the pavement, the men in their serge suits and flat caps and the women in their factory uniforms. A woman in a beige gabardine joins her at the stop, pulls a compact from her handbag and starts powdering her face. For some reason Berry the farmer suddenly crosses her mind. She thinks about the ice on the well and the fields of frost-tipped mud. Another bus pulls up, growls and moves away. Another woman in a gabardine coat crosses the road and begins to make her way towards Plaistow Wharf. Jenny thinks about how much there is to lose on either side. London, a husband. The woman powdering her face smiles, walks in front, and clambers on to the number 101.

And suddenly it hits her. Of course, the gabardine coats. A job lot loosened from a lorry. Cheap, they are, and second rate. She rushes on to the bus, jangling her pocket for change and thinking, Oh Len Page, you've really been and gone and done it now.

CHAPTER 21

I ain't even took me rollers out yet, says Olive Walter, opening the door to Jenny. But never mind, come in and have a cuppa, pet. I got them fig biscuits you like.

Jenny steps into the hallway of the tiny house in Parker Street, Silvertown, not as easily as she once did, the arthritis having crept into her hips and travelled to her knees now.

I'll put the kettle on, says Olive, waving her friend to the tweed settee.

Since that evening long ago in Lyle Park, Jenny has become friends with the Walters, first Bill then his sister. She sits, and the brindle greyhound Bill took on after Bosun died lifts his head from its place by the gas fire and thumps its tail. The clock on the mantel chimes quarter past four.

Bill's off on one of his meetings, says Olive. Local housing, park maintenance, traffic jams, you know the sort of thing. He'll be back shortly.

Jenny rearranges the tubigrip around her knees and waits. She looks around the room, with its beige wallpaper, its portraits of the Queen and the Princess Royal and the engraving of the *Mauritania*, its parrot in a cage, its dog with the slowly flapping tail. Her legs ache, her hands are like chicken feet, her stomach rumbles and churns. She is sixty-five but feels much older.

So how are you, Jenny? Olive shouts from the kitchen.

Been better. Jenny is hoping this teasing response will stretch into a discussion of her aches and pains, the tubigrip, the nightmarish condition of her stomach, because these are the things she likes talking about now. But no, Olive merely asks her to repeat herself. It's easy to forget her friend's deafness because she talks so much. It strikes Jenny that this may be why she talks so much. She doesn't have to listen to herself.

Been better, Olive.

After Olive's husband was killed on the western front, she went to work as a conductor on the buses. When her hips made standing up all day impossible, she got a 'little job' in the administrative department of Crosse and Blackwell, then moved to Tate and Lyle's, filing purchase orders. Since then, she and her brother have lived an unassuming life, grateful for what is theirs – steady employment, a small nest-egg under the mattress, the allotment where Bill grows vegetables and dahlias, an assortment of disused greyhounds and a talking parrot. Bill has his local meetings, his liaison committees and lobbying groups, and Olive has her crochet.

Jenny begins playing with the denture glue in her upper plate and looks around for a sweet. She spies a little pile of barley sugars in a dish, leans forwards and pinches one, quickly, before Olive comes back.

Oh, haven't we all, pet? shouts Olive from the kitchen. Still, never mind, eh? She bustles in, minus her rollers, carrying a tray with tea. I've put out a few dry to have with your wet, she says, placing the tea tray on the table at the side of the room and arranging the fig biscuits on a plate. How are you getting on in *that place?*

She means Shell at Charing Cross, where Jenny works as a waitress in the staff canteen.

Oh, I can't complain, says Jenny. But she can, of course. She can.

Len was amazed and bewildered by his wife's refusal to leave London, but he set up home in Hampshire all the same. The South Essex flats of his childhood were all built up and it was the country he was after. In Len's mind he'd have a better quality of life out west. For six months he assumed Jenny would relent and follow him, and when she didn't he gave up on her. With June and Harry he set up a transport café on the Staines to Basingstoke Road, the A33, and called it The Shack, because that was what it was.

With Len gone and The Cosy Corner Café closed, my grand-mother contemplated a return to the tailoring trade, but it was too late, her hands were too stiff to manage the fabric and her eyes were not good enough to follow a line. Oh it wasn't so bad, waitressing. She liked the company at Shell and for the first time in her life she was in control of her money. It wasn't a lot of money but it was truly and completely hers, and that alone made it seem like riches.

I don't think Jenny blamed Len for leaving, there was no point. Their marriage had probably been doomed from the first, she thinks now. She's not given to introspection but she does occasionally wonder how different her life might have been had she refused to return to Altmore Avenue on that morning after the wedding. There had seemed so few choices. She and Len were terribly ill-matched. They had been drawn together only because they each wanted to move on. Over the years Jenny had tried to do a few alterations on Len but it was no use, he was unalterable. Len, in turn, had tried to weave her into some other shape but she was too inflexible.

She had been a good wife, if not a loving one. She'd done the necessary – cooked his tea, whitened his step, sewn his clothes and borne his children, and his fist. When he had left she had felt washed up and bitter, her only consolations sherbet lemons and mint cracknells and Olive and Bill. And London, of course. Sometimes she forgot how much she loved London. Asking her to leave it was like asking her to leave herself. Impossible.

Jenny Page is chewing on a fig biscuit as Bill Walter bounds in through the front door. Ah, he cries, if it ain't me second favourite bird. How are you, Jenny pet? (For years she was Mrs P, but now she is always Jenny pet.)

Hello, shrieks the parrot. Bill runs his fingers along its head.

Good meeting? Olive spoons three sugar cubes into her brother's tea, stirs and shoots him a disapproving look.

Oh, you know, says Bill, them towerblocks again. Olive does not share her brother's enthusiasm for towerblocks. Over and over again they have the same argument.

Whass someone like me, bad hips, gonna do in a towerblock?

They got *lifts*, Olive pet.

What if the lifts don't *work*.

But they *do*, Olive pet. You got to adapt, you got to develop, see?

Says who?

Says the council.

And when did you ever listen to the council, Bill Walter?

They fall silent. For a moment the only sound in the room comes from Jenny's dentures negotiating the biscuit. Bill picks up his tea and slides into a tweed armchair by the gas fire.

Did Olive mention our holiday? he says, changing the subject. We're reckoning to go down to Butlins at Bognor for a week. Thought you might swing along, pet.

Jenny considers the Butlins promise: the cooked meals, the Old

Time dance halls, the Entertainers, Arthur English, Tommy Steele, the Pig and Whistle bars, the home from home atmosphere.

I'll take that as a yes then, he says, helping himself to another cup of tea.

They got *lifts*, hisses the parrot.

Jenny walks back to the bus stop at a slow pace, past the Socialist Dockers' Club and the dark terraces with their outfitting of smuts, each little house leaning in on its neighbours in toxic comradeship, like a row of hopeless drunks. Most have been condemned and are awaiting slum clearance, and many of the old residents have already left and are living in prefabs beside Bow Creek and in Beckton. She passes Tate's Social. Behind her towers the Lyle's Golden Syrup factory at Plaistow Wharf, only three years old when The Cosy Corner Café first opened but already worn soft by the acid fumes from the Union Mills on one side and John Knight's animal rendering plant on the other.

So much has changed in Silvertown since Len left. Factories have gone up and rows of efficient-looking red-brick council houses have replaced the worst of the Victorian terraces. There are new transit sheds and refrigerated warehouses along the northside of the Victoria and Albert Docks, and a new lock is planned for the western end of the Vic. A little further along there are new storage tanks for petroleum at Shell and a new biscuit factory at Tay Wharf.

For all that, Silvertown seems forgotten by the rest of the East End. Elsewhere in this part of London you can sense the beginnings of other worlds, experiments in planning and development and new ways of living, the separation of the urban mass into residential, commercial and industrial zones. Where belching chimneys once abutted workers' cottages and parades of dingy shops, there are now industrial estates and shopping centres. Council estates cover vast areas that ten years before were striped with bombed-out streets and rubble. Arterial roads chop through old market areas and pre-fabricated offices house the headquarters of the social services and labour exchange. Only in Silvertown do the shops and cafés and social clubs and houses and schools still cling to the docks and factory walls like wet flags to a pole.

Her feet take her west. Through a gap in a factory wall the bulking Mammoth crane appears out on the river by the West Ham Wharf, edging a vast cube of machinery, a boiler perhaps, across the water towards the quay. She reaches for a sweet in her bag and is unexpectedly hit by a sudden sense of hollowness. Poor Silvertown. She remembers the days when she and Dora called it the sugar mile.

For the first time in her life, Jenny lives alone now. It is nearly thirteen years since Hanny and Red helped her ex-husband move his things from the house in Altmore Avenue. Is this all, guv? There wasn't much. A few clothes, a tool box for his motor, his old army uniform and boots, his ARP buckle and badge, his dog trophies. He took his book of clippings from *Greyhound Life* and the pictures of his dogs. Everything else he left. Len was never much of a man for homeliness and domesticity. For most of his life he had lived in exile.

Years pass. She doesn't count them. She still thinks in tides, half a day at a time. The future is too vast and chaotic. Why think about the future when the past is so unmanageable?

She goes to work on the number 15. She comes back from work on the number 15, she cooks herself a bit of tea, visits Dora every so often, lays flowers in the East London cemetery on the anniversaries of her parents' deaths. She eats sweets and crochets antimacassars for the neighbours' Christmas presents. She still sews, though mostly tea cosies and aprons. At weekends she'll take the bus down to the Rathbone Market in Canning Town because they do nice offcuts of bacon and sometimes there is a Jew-boy selling cheap fabric, buttons and other haberdashery, only you can't call them Jew-boys now. Her marriage is a tick buried deep in her skin. Weeks will go by and she will hardly think of it, then one day she will wake in the night and feel it burning in a part of her body she has no words for, a pain she cannot voice. And then that too fades. Her life is occupied and peaceful, if a little lonely. She watches television. Most of the time she just gets on with things.

In May 1968, while students throw Molotov cocktails, Bill and Olive Walter and Jenny Page sit on a bus to Butlins Holiday Camp in Bognor Regis, eating paste sandwiches and singing the Butlins song.

Come all you scholars now and put away your studies,
Come and join the happy band, known as the Butlins Buddies.

Crab or fish? says Bill, who is in a buoyant mood.
I always make fish, his sister says. You know that.
Not crab is it? says Bill. Can't stick crab.
The coach slows around a bend and swerves to avoid a cyclist in the middle of the road. The three of them lurch forward in their seats, grabbing on to their plastic cups and sandwich wrappers.
A crab can't help being a crab, says Jenny, dabbing at spilt lemonade.
Well I appreciate that, you see, says Bill, wiping his hands on his trousers. But that don't mean I have to like it.
Mebbe it don't like you much either, Bill Walter, says Olive. I know I don't.
They fall silent for a while, crossing the South Downs by Arundel. For a moment the bus peers down over the cathedral and the castle with its rocky surround and red battlements.

We're a bit like a sandwich ourselfs when you think about it, says Olive. Sitting in this bus with the country on either side.

Not a crab sandwich, says Bill.

Have it your way, says Olive.

I will, says Bill.

By the time the bus pulls into the iron gates of the holiday camp it is beginning to rain. Jenny and Olive don their plastic hats to protect their newly-rollered hair. A redcoat appears to show them to their chalets. Hoorah, says Bill, helping the women from the bus. Ain't this something?

The chalets are in a row of about twenty located in the quiet section of the camp at right angles to the Golden Grill and the Beachcomber Bar. The front windows look out across a small patch of worn, brown grass to a row of similar chalets strung along the other side of the walkway. Bizzy lizzies and pink geraniums bloom beside the litter bins. A miniature train runs around the perimeter, ferrying Butlins Buddies from the billiard room to the crazy golf course, and from the Golden Grill to the Pig and Whistle pub. Inside each chalet is a bed, a desk and chair, a basin and a cupboard, the whole decorated in jolly pastels with pictures of yachts on the walls. A map of the complex stapled to the back of the door shows 'You are Here' in red felt-tip lettering.

This is nice, Olive says. Different, but not too different.

Righty-ho, I'll leave you to it, beams the redcoat. Don't forget there's trampoline practice and bingo at half past two. Hi-de-hi.

Very dainty, Jenny says. What are we supposed to do, again?

Have fun, says Bill.

After tea in the Grill they take the miniature train around the compound. By now it is raining hard so they sit in the social club for a few hours reading the papers and magazines until it's time for more tea. Bill follows the Indian waiter with his eyes.

That was an ugly business in the docks last month, he says, once the man is out of earshot. Watching them dockers marchin' up and down, women too, mouthin' that hateful rubbish. They should be ashamed.

There's a lot of coloureds about, says Olive.

Ah, what does bloody Enoch Powell know? Let him come down to the East End and see for hisself. Bleedn politicians. There'll be a river of blood, my arse. If the Thames ain't already a river of blood! The industrialists and the unions are fighting one another like butchers' dogs over a bone and all the time the docks are goin' to hell and taking the East End with 'em.

Only three years earlier, in 1965, London was still the largest port in the world, and one of the busiest. In the early Sixties, Silver City, the largest covered shed in Europe, had been built at the Royal Victoria Dock. That was how much faith everyone had. By 1968 it looked like an act of enormous hubris. The innermost dock of the Upper Pool, St Katharine's, had just closed, and the previous year the new Brunswick Power Station had been built over the site of the East India. The newspapers were saying the West India would be next to close. The speed of these closures had left East Enders breathless and it was easier to blame poor men in turbans than to engage with the complex and debilitating idea that they had been let down by politicians, industrialists and unions; in other words, by every agency which claimed to be able to protect them.

Another cup of tea anyone? says Olive finally. No sense in being gloomy. Bill leans over and pats his sister's arm. Who's game for the bingo?

Jenny wakes the following morning to the sound of the camp tannoy requesting campers to roll out of bed with a great big smile. She opens the curtains to see rain smashing against the window. After breakfast in the Golden Grill they join in a beetle drive and

after a post-lunch nap they are at the bingo. The Walters fall to
their cards, frantically marking the numbers as they're called: two
fat ladies, eighty-eight, snake eyes, eleven, three-oh, thirty. But
Jenny lets her mind drift. Twenty-four, dad at the door, eighty-two,
hole in me shoe, forty-four, mouth is sore, seventy-eight, the house
in a state, number four, being poor. What a life it has been. The
scent of Bill's hair tonic hits her. Twenty-two, me and you. Twenty-
three, you and me.

They pass their final evening at Butlins at the Old Time dance
in the ballroom. Jenny wears a homemade crimplene dress with
imitation pearls around her neck and in her ears. She thinks of
Rosie and Dora and what they would say if they saw her now. How
much they would smile. She kisses her lips with raspberry lipstick.
There.

Look at you, whistles Bill. A right picture.

Ah, now, Bill Walter, keep a hold on yerself, she says, embarrassed.

He winks at her and, taking both women by the arm, says, Let's
go then, ladies.

As they walk along the concrete path towards the ballroom, past
the hullabaloo of the swimming pool and the children's playground,
they feel as though they are floating above it all in some quiet,
enchanted bubble. Sitting at the tropical bar overhung with plastic
pineapples in leather seats reclaimed from wartime fighter planes,
they sip on sherries and admire the vast ballroom mirrors that once
were the insides of search lights. A twelve-piece band begins a swing
number and to Jenny Page some other life momentarily opens up
and offers itself.

Come on, old girl, let's have a dance, says Bill.

Oh no, Bill, I can't.

Yes you can, Jenny Page, says Bill, pulling her out of her chair,
and you're just about to.

She stands with her arms plastered to her sides while the band strikes up the 'Chattanooga Choo Choo'.

C'mon, says Bill, pushing her gently towards the dance floor, and she suddenly feels herself smiling and a moment after that Bill's arm snakes around her skinny waist, his broad hand clamps hers and they are off, shuffling about the floor and avoiding each other's gaze.

This is the life, pet, ain't it?

She feels herself, stiff as a board, swaying in his arms.

You know, he says, we could have done this years ago. What ninnies we are!

I ain't much of a dancer, she says, stepping on Bill's toe.

Never too late to learn.

They paddle their way around the room again, gazing out into the middle distance, hanging on grimly. Tomorrow or next year she'll forget all this. She'll forget because it will hurt to remember.

All too soon it's over and they are trundling back to London on the bus, ignoring the green smears of country around them, full up as they are with private thoughts. Halfway through the journey they unwrap their sandwiches. Bill turns a piece of Mother's Pride over in his hand.

Is this crab or fish?

The first hint they have of London is the smell. It pours through the air vents in the bus. Before long they are stuttering across the city itself, through neat, hedge-trimmed southern suburbs towards the broad thread of the river. The bus drops them and their bags at Victoria Station.

How much would a cab to the East End be? asks Olive.

Too much, says Jenny.

They clamber on to the bus and ten minutes later find themselves curling around Buckingham Palace and along the side of St James's Park. Olive checks her watch.

'Ere, do you think the Queen is having her tea?

Course not, says Jenny, laughing.

Why not?

Because Royals are Royals. They don't eat the same or think the same or do the same as us.

What do they eat? says Olive.

Crab bloody sandwiches, says Bill.

They sail on east towards the City, the West End vanishing behind them. At the Bow Road they have to change buses. For ten minutes they stand at the bus stop outside Kelly's before the salt smell of fried fish finally overcomes them.

I don't mind being a commoner if you can stop and 'ave fish and chips at Kelly's, says Bill, stabbing at the batter with his little wooden fork. They immerse themselves in the pleasure of the softly flaking cod with its crisp, oily jacket and accompanying salted chips.

'Ere, says Olive, clearing a space in her pile of chips, just shows how fresh these chips is, they're on this evening's paper.

Anything exciting happen while we was away? asks Bill.

I dunno, says Olive, it's the sports section.

Her brother reaches for the Woolworth's glasses in his shirt pocket and peers closer at his paper wrap. In the passing of a second his face turns as dun as gutter water. Christ all-bloody-mighty. Mary mother of God.

At dawn on 16 May 1968, a gas cooker exploded on the eighteenth floor of a 200ft-high towerblock at Ronan Point, Canning Town. In the space of a few minutes, the entire eastern corner of the towerblock collapsed, sending dressing tables, electric fires, chairs and sofas hurtling to the ground below. Five men and women were killed outright, crushed by concrete or else suffocated in the dust. Eleven more were seriously injured. The building had been occupied less than two months.

The towerblock was one of four identical blocks in a single slum clearance contract between the borough of Newham (West Ham and East Ham collectively) and Taylor Woodrow. Built using the new Swedish Larsen-Nielsen system, the towerblocks at Ronan Point had promised a solution to the problem of cheap, decent housing in the East End. Where the two-up-two-downs were hutches advertising their poverty, the new towers were advertisements for a clean and modern way of living, a modern way of being, a permanent and affordable solution to the Abyss. They were sold to the public as palaces in the sky.

All over the East End the traditional grids of streets and corner shops vanished in favour of concrete walkways and vast, twenty-two-storey residential skyscrapers. A great architecture of alienation grew up, almost as disordered and grim as the shambling little alleys and turnings of a hundred years before, and even more fragile. When Ronan Point collapsed, the whole well-intentioned, ill-conceived compromise that had become the post-war East End fell with it. Ronan Point was more than a failed towerblock. It was where the dream of a new East End came to a crumbling halt.

CHAPTER 22

Jenny shuffles over the little wooden step into the corner shop at the top of Altmore Avenue. The smells of cardamom and cumin meet her at the entrance. Inside, warm air is blowing from a heated fan by the cash till and a plump woman in a sari is filling some shelves with tins of minced meat. Christmas is approaching and the puny plastic Christmas tree Jenny recalls from the year before is sitting on the till.

Afternoon, Mrs Page, says the plump woman.

Jenny moves along the rows of Vespa curry boxes and packets of crisps. What she wants to say is Good Afternoon, Mrs Ranavand-rum, how are you doing, and how is your bonny daughter, Narinda Ranavandrum, and your sweet little boy, Sahel Ranavandrum, and what about your helpful husband, Waheed Ranavandrum? But she can't say any of it in case her teeth pop out. This is no idle fear. She did once try saying Ranavandrum in front of the mirror and out they came. Since then, the fear of saying Ranavandrum has become so overwhelming that she has to avoid speaking to the Ranavandrums or even making eye contact with them. All the same, the Ranavandrums' shop is very handy and Olive and Bill are coming for tea and she has nothing but a few stale malted milk biscuits in the house. What she needs is Battenburg cake. She creeps behind the chocolate counter, heading for the section beside the Rich Tea biscuits. She calculates that she has about thirty seconds before Mrs Ranavandrum comes looking for her, offering help.

The Battenburgs are in their normal place. She reaches out, but at that very moment there is a swishing sound and Mrs Ranavandrum's sari appears around the corner.

You looking for anything in particular?

Jenny smiles and lifts the cake.

Ah, says Mrs Ranavandrum. Guests for tea?

Jenny nods in the most friendly way she can muster. Mrs Ranavandrum will think she's simple.

A special occasion is it? asks Mrs R, and getting no answer, adds, No? Well, come over to the counter and I'll get you a bag to put it in.

Jenny takes a packet of sherbet lemons off the shelf by the till then hands over a few coins to cover both the sweets and the cake.

You've given me too much, says Mrs Ranavandrum. It's this new currency, isn't it? Hard to remember.

Jenny puts the cake in her plastic tote and does a quick calculation of the cost in the old money, which is what she understands.

Have a good day, Mrs Page, says Mrs Ranavandrum.

Thank you, says Jenny, surging from the shop.

On the way back to number 27, she thinks about Len and wonders if he ever regretted leaving the East End. She doesn't think so. She hurries past the phone box and notices that someone has sprayed it with BNP graffiti and smashed the coin box. Then she turns into her familiar road, not so familiar now. The polled trees are thicker than they used to be, the post boxes scruffier, and the corner shops are mostly owned by Asians. Even the houses look different now. In the last twenty years little porches have been added, and stone cladding, and here and there a modern door with patterned, frosted glass.

Home is the same damp corner it has always been. Some plastic flowers in a vase on the mantel brighten the place up. She has some pretty new whatnots – a porcelain squirrel eating a nut, a shire horse, a stoneware girl chasing a butterfly, a clock made from engraved copper and a spider plant in a plastic pot – but no amassed quantity of gewgaws and china gobbets and plastic bits and pieces can give the old place anything approaching a lift.

Jenny sits the Battenburg on a chipped flowered plate, puts out her best tea set and waits for Bill and Olive. They will be late, of course, and Olive will complain about the reduction in the bus services from Silvertown, as she always does. To be fair on Olive she has a point. It's the same story across the East End – reductions in bus services, clinics, libraries, schools, rubbish disposal, housing services, street sweeping, the lot.

It has been six years now since the East India Dock at Black-wall closed. Soon the Millwall and West India Docks will go too. Though no one knows this yet, the Royals are also doomed. The Royal Victoria Dock in Silvertown will take in its last ship in the early 1980s. In 1981 all commercial shipping in the Royal Albert and King George V Docks will cease. The last vessel to be loaded in the Royals will leave the KGV on 7 October 1981. The final cargo ever to be discharged there will come off ship three weeks later.

Only a decade or so before, Silvertown Way had been called the road to the Empire. An atmosphere of denial had prevailed. In 1967 a new lock was even built at the western end of the Vic. The Fred Olsen shipping line spent a million pounds on a passenger ferry terminal at the West India. But it was all too late. The western lock was never used and the ferry terminal was closed not long after it opened.

Over the course of the next few years dozens of shops, fish and chippies, cafés, eel stalls, pawnbrokers, ships' chandlers, uniform-makers, post offices, bookies, cinemas, dockers' clubs, launderettes, ropemakers, seamen's missions, currency exchanges, gambling dens and pubs all closed. The areas adjacent to the West and East India, Millwall and the Royal Docks became more or less derelict, a place for discarded dogs and abandoned cars. The drained marshes that had for centuries been home to factories and billowing chimney stacks turned into a dumping ground, and its towerblocks degener-ated into dirty, run-down dives for families the council didn't know what else to do with. To the disenfranchised poor of Wapping, Shadwell, Limehouse, Poplar, Blackwall, Canning Town and Sil-vertown, life was little better than it had been for their grandparents in the Abyss.

In the late Fifties, 250,000 men made their living inside the dock walls. By the early Seventies, 10,000 men were on the dole around the docks, and by the early Eighties, 80,000 men would be without work. No history book can adequately describe the rush, the fury almost, with which this decline happened. Fork lift trucks replaced dockers' hooks and new cranes came in which could lift heavier cargoes on to the quay in greater bulk than before. Wider ships' hatches made the handling of cargo in the hold easier. Palletisation reduced the need for manual labour even further and the introduction of containers more or less eliminated it. Of the London ports only Tilbury, thirteen miles downstream, was able to service con-tainer ships. Then cargo was consolidated into standard units and roll-on/roll-off ships were built which unloaded directly on to the quayside. Refrigerated trucks became cheaper and more efficient, so meat and other perishables were taken to cold stores outside the docks and nearer to distribution points. The grand mills emptied – Ranks, Spillers, the Cooperative Wholesale Society – made redun-dant by discharge vacuum pumps that sucked the grain from bulk carriers at Tilbury. Downstream it all went. Eastwards, with the tide.

The East End spluttered like a man with half a lung. There were protests, of course, and occasional strikes. The unions brought their men out, muttered, horsetraded, and brought their men out again. In 1971 five union men were arrested and slung in Pentonville Prison for blacking vehicles bypassing the docks. There were mass meetings in Victoria Park. One hundred and seventy thousand dockers from all over the country went out on sympathy strike for the Pentonville Five. If you had looked hard enough you would have seen Hanny and Red in there among the crowd.

A few dockers agreed to be transferred to Tilbury, others got redundancy payouts, bought timeshare villas in Spain or set up local businesses destined to fail in the economy of decline. A few made good, joined the Cockney diaspora and found themselves breathing the thin, elevated air of the middle classes in places like Ongar and Billericay. But most did not. Shipwrecked and bewildered, they lined up at the dole offices, reminiscent of the Sally Army soup kitchens half a century before. A few of the younger men, whose redundancy payments were low and prospects of re-employment small, took it out on whoever was convenient, thumping their way around pubs and clubs, heads shaved and boots polished until, realising the fruitlessness of their cause, they grew quiet and middle-aged.

Their children grew up in the empty spaces while their parents told them tales of how the river had burned brilliant yellow during the war and how you could walk all the way across the water on the lighters moored midstream. The children laughed, enchanted and disbelieving. By the late 1980s, almost the only evidence that there had ever been a dock in Poplar, in Millwall, in Blackwall, in Silvertown, in North Woolwich, was to be found on the name plaques of luxury residential developments inhabited by bankers, which cynically proclaimed their authenticity by calling themselves Cinnamon Wharf or Ivory Dock. A few of the older warehouses and customs houses and dockmasters' houses were preserved, but whole areas of the docks became deserted, post-industrial wastelands scoured by the westerlies that blew in from the city.

In the midst of all this Jenny sits and waits for her old friends. Were she an activist, she might write a letter of protest, lobby her MP, but she has rarely stood up for herself. Her life has been fight enough.

The kettle is singing when the doorbell rings, and there on the doorstep are Bill clutching his hat and Olive clutching a pile of her crocheted antimacassars, neither knowing what to say.

The kettle's on, says Jenny.

Lovely, says Olive.

Jenny takes their coats and shows them through to the kitchen.

And, so, how, er, *are* you? begins Olive, creeping across the sentence as though it were land mined.

Jenny shakes the linen tablecloth from the drawer in the cupboard and spreads it out on Frenchie's table.

She brings in the teapot and the cake.

Oo, Battenburg, my favourite, says Olive.

No it ain't, says Bill.

Ignoring her brother, Olive says, 'So will you be, em, you know . . . ?

Jenny pours the tea into china cups. That's already seen to, she says. She feels oddly detached, as though her head is floating above the plate of cake. *She's* seen to it, she says. It was her what signed the death certificate.

Len Page died on 8 December 1973 in Hampshire. Half a century of heavy smoking had taken its toll. The cancer had spread through his lungs and the drugs they gave him had addled his brain. He played out the final months and weeks of his life in a hospital bed, incoherent and meandering, stumbling into a darkness that no charming smile, no ducking or diving and no slowly turning fist could keep out. It was then that I met him for the first time. I was seven. He was quite a shocking sight, to a child, anyway. His breath was heavy and forced, his hair bleached and yellowed by tobacco smoke, his skin like an omelette. I remember him talking about violins or violinists but he must have been hallucinating. He was dying as best he could, unforgiving and unforgiven. Of all the ways people die, that is probably the worst. He was rarely spoken about on my side of the family. It was concluded that he had caused too much pain to be much mourned. All the same, I think Jenny must, to some degree at least, have understood why he did what he did, why he had to do it. They were born into worlds that shared the same low horizon. The difference between them was that Lenny wanted something better for himself. And somewhere in her heart Jenny did not begrudge him that.

What a lovely Christmas tree, says Olive, admiring the little pot of green on the floor by the gas fire. They have been talking about Princess Anne and Prince Charles and how much they look forward to the Queen's Christmas speech and how lovely the royal family always look on telly. The conversation meanders on, skirting any further mention of Len.

Well, says Olive, finally, I suppose we'd better be going. You know what the buses are like.

While Olive shuffles out to use the privy, Bill and Jenny are left together, on opposite sides of Frenchie Fulcher's table, contemplating the remains of the cake.

Jenny, says Bill, ain't there nothing I can do to change your mind, old girl?

She shrugs and sucks harder on the sherbet lemon in her mouth.

Have a sherbet lemon, she says.

Bill shoves another piece of Battenburg in his mouth to shut himself up or stop himself from crying. He leans over and pats her head. They both know it's no use. Jenny is one of those war weeds struggling among the rubble, a small sprout of rosebay willow herb, deeply rooted, pushing up its thin stems towards the light and every so often throwing out a straggly flower. But her heart is still down there in the rubble.

It has grown dark by the time Jenny shows her old friends out. Whenever they say their goodbyes at the door now it is with the understanding that each goodbye may be a last. Olive kisses her friend on the cheek and pats her hair. Bill puts an arm around her waist and kisses her lightly on the lips. And a sweet kiss it is too, but not as sweet as the taste of sherbet lemons.

Epilogue

I have often wandered around Silvertown, trying to find the traces left by Jenny and Len Page. I got there too late for The Cosy Corner Café. It has long since disappeared. Where it once stood there is now a housing estate.

Silvertown has changed so much that it is difficult to visualise the place it was in the Forties and Fifties when Len plotted his escape. The London Docklands Development Corporation retained some of the old dockside cranes, the swing bridge at the western entrance of the Royal Vic, a few cast-iron capstans and some carefully selected late-Victorian warehousing, but that is all. The Thames Flood Barrier just west of Tate and Lyle's has taken over from the Lea as the point where London ends and the rest of the river is left to itself. No one seems to mind if Silvertown floods because there is so little left to get wet. The bulking Seamen's Mission at Custom House has been converted into a student hostel. South of where the Victoria Dock once stood, the stucco shell of the Millennium Flour Mills and, behind it, hard up against North Woolwich Way, the white tower of grain silo 'D' both await a bright idea for redevelopment. There is a new system of roundabouts and bypasses, complete with choking traffic and neat, tangential flyovers. People no longer come to the Royals so much as drive right through them. To the north, the Docklands Light Railway rattles by, past the Peacock boxing gym at Canning Town, where working boys convert to fighting flesh, and the Britannia Flag, where they revert to flab again.

Often my walks through Silvertown end at City Airport, which was opened in 1986 on the old site of the Albert Dock. The runway is the dividing quay between what used to be the Royal Albert and the King George V Docks. I sit in the tearoom and watch the planes move across the stilled waters of the ex-dock, while skylarks work the tepid flare of jets. Once I wandered along the north side and picked blackberries, prematurely ripened in the exhaust fumes. Another time I came on two boys diving off Connaught Bridge, leaving divots in the water where they landed.

Some debris of the past remains. St Mark's Church is still there, surrounded by razor wire, and until very recently Tate and Lyle's Plaistow Wharf still stood, barely changed since the 1930s. Opposite is the corner where Johnny Donal protested his dismissal for twenty-six years. Many of the noxious industries are still there. The spent bodies of cattle are still being ground up at John Knight's. Along the riverine strip there is still a pitch lake and petroleum tanks and a paint factory.

In 1994, Jenny started to give away her sweets. I sensed she was dying. It was a long, drawn-out death. I know because I witnessed it. Edie, John and Frances Maud had all died long before. I don't know what happened to Arthur. I don't think he and Jenny were in touch. Dora died in Essex. Once she and the Walters became too frail to travel, Jenny wrote to Bill and Olive every week, sometimes twice a week, until at last her letters were no longer returned. One by one, the pieces of her life fell away.

Looking back, I think she struggled to leave her life because she had never squeezed a good deal from it. Life had roundly ripped her off. Her last days were spent in a nursing home. You had to shout at her because she was deaf, and virtually blind, too. The doctor said she had peripheral vision and couldn't see anything that was right in front of her. To the last she crept around the edges of her days, and was as I had always known her – tiny, sour and righteously defensive. She lived in a more or less permanent state of self-pity and was subject to impossibly prickly moods.

So there she was, at ninety-one, a tiny woman with no teeth who had borne two children but had never seen a naked man; a woman who had been born in London but had never visited the Tower or St Paul's; a woman who would not talk to her local shopkeeper in case she had to pronounce her name. But a woman whose strong sense of place it is hard for me to imagine. Jenny Fulcher was someone who *belonged*.

Acknowledgements

I have wanted to write this book for a long time, but the impetus to start rose out of an article I wrote for the *Guardian* in 1997. Deborah Orr commissioned that article and without her, I doubt *Silvertown* would ever have seen the light of day. Among those who helped in the early stages by sharing their expertise and their experiences were Dick Hobbs, Bill Fishmann, Graham Hurley, Grace Beckford, Ingrid Carroll, Howard Bloch, Iain Sinclair and Bill Dunlop. Later, when I was working on what was to become the text for this book, the librarians at Tower Hamlets and Stratford local history libraries were very helpful, as were Anthony Sampson, Julia Rae, Brian Nicholson, Mary Mills, Vic Turner, Chris Elmers and Bob Aspinall at the Museum of Docklands, Bill and Davy Grainger, Ron Armitage and others at the Royal Oak, North Woolwich, and Michael Greer and Eileen Guyver at Tate and Lyle.

Tai Bridgeman has been a true friend and a great source of support. Adrian Gatton renewed my passion for the subject and saw me through the final, most difficult stages. To the many others who encouraged and supported me over what proved to be a long journey, thank you. Without your friendship I would have floundered.

My agent, David Godwin, has been tremendous. I owe a great debt of gratitude to my editor Nicholas Pearson and to Nick Davies who put in a huge amount of work on the manuscript, to Rachel

Connelly who was an exemplary copyeditor and to everyone at Fourth Estate who believed in the book and assisted in its creation.

Greatest thanks go to my family, without whom neither this book nor its author would ever have come into being.

Some of the names of people in this book have been changed to protect their privacy.